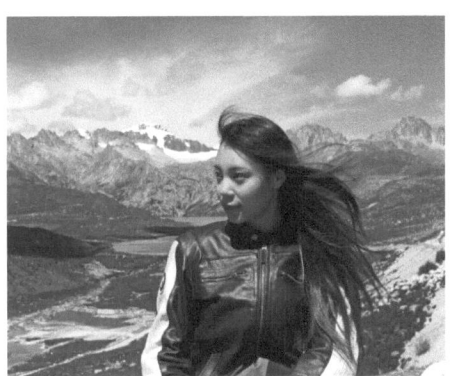

Sonia.Shuang WU

1986   Born in Chongqing Municipality, China
2005-2009   Oil Painting, Sichuan Fine Arts Institute, China
2007   Free Art, Kassel University, Germany
2009   B.A of Sichuan Fine Arts Institute
2014   Post-graduate （M.A）, Central Academy of Fine Arts (CAFA), China
Currently lives and works in Beijing China

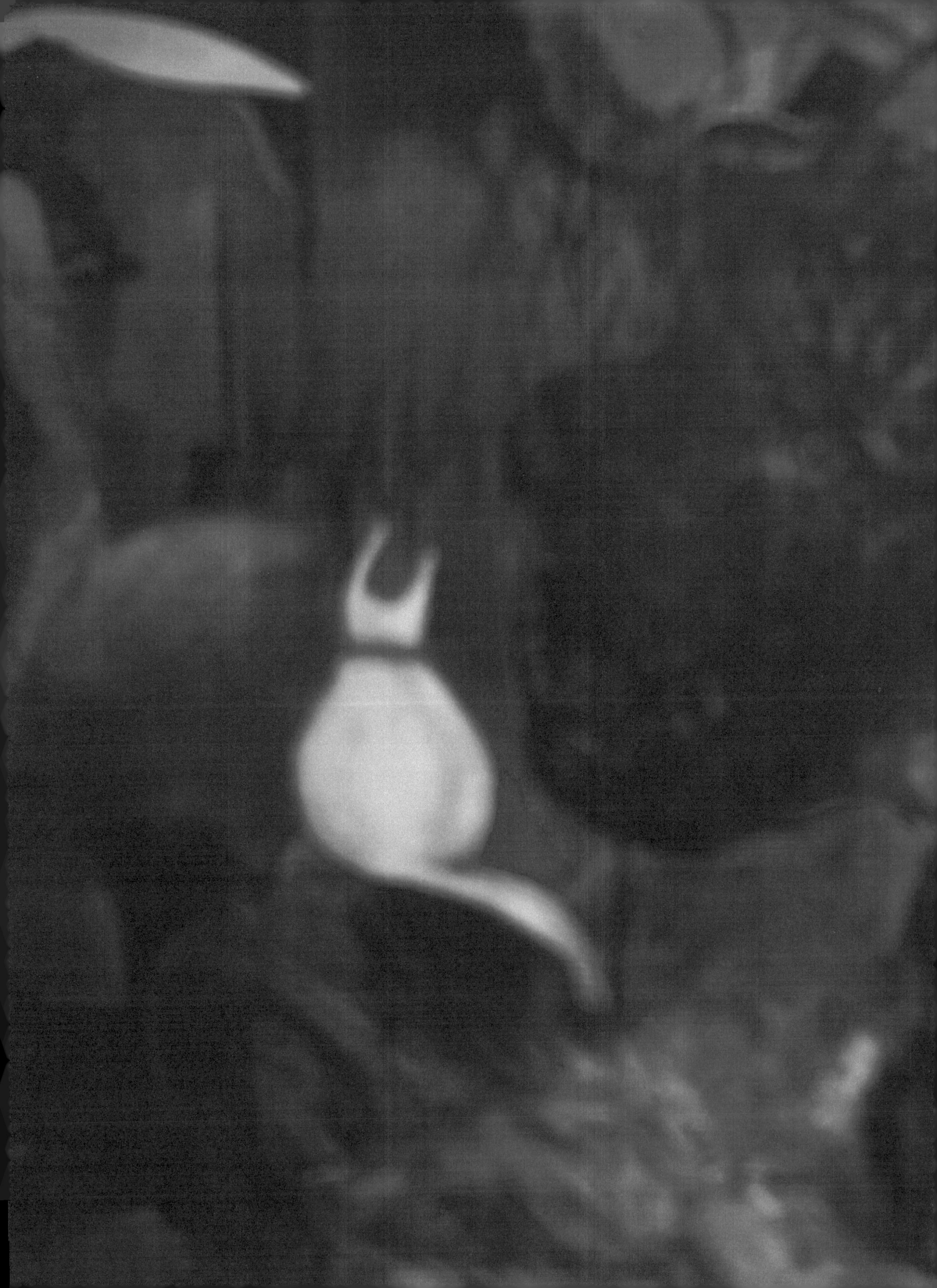

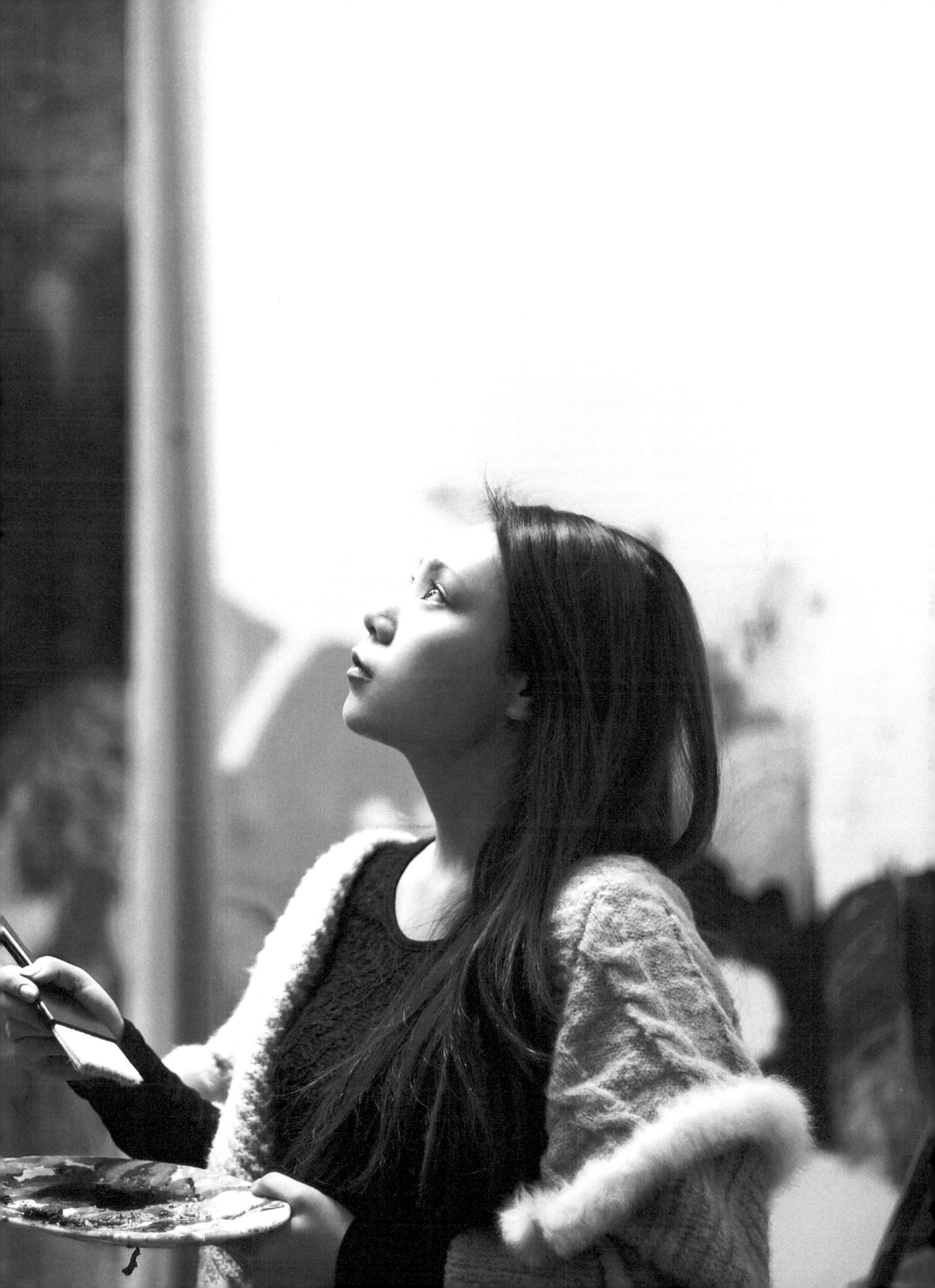

Preface

A responsibility Of great importance fell on me when Wu Shuang invited me to deliver the preface a few days ago. As her intimate friend who has been with her for the past 20 years, I will speak, with great familiarity, on her talents in painting that was displayed since she was little.

She became attached to painting since she was a little girl. She was admitted into Nankai high school as an art specialty student. Her admission into Sichuan Fine Arts Institute brought her a turning point where she began to have a deeper thinking about and understanding of art and life. Starting as an innocent student, she made great progress by holding an exhibition "Activation" in 2008 in 4 years during which I saw her interpreting the initial thinking about colors of life. The works on show included "······Born" (2008), "Save mother" (2008), "Let's grow up together! My darling woman" (2008) and others. Female pregnancy is a mission required by social norms. A 10-month life cycle can be as long as a journey, a love and a short-term job or many other meaningful things where more experience and value are generated. Nonetheless, a 10-month pregnancy takes up a woman's everything in her body, time and energy. All the attention paid to women and the thinking about and allegation of value of their existence appear vividly on her works.

Her artistic creation comes from her experience and understanding of life. In 2007, she obtained the only quota offered by Sichuan Fine Arts Institute to be an exchange student with her all-round excellences. She went to Germany-based University of Kassel alone where she absorbed the western culture as possible as she could. She traveled through all the museums, art galleries and libraries in Europe during extracurricular time and vocations. She traveled enthusiastically through all the countries around Mediterranean Sea to feel the local folk customs. She benefited a lot from the mental shock from European avant-garde art as well as the impact between western social ideology and eastern way of thinking. Her living abroad on her own was more about harvest than stress and helplessness. Learning tour opened a broader door of art to her, which launched her thinking about and exploration into feminism from 2007 to 2009. Infusing the speculation of feminism into her graduation thesis helped her win the excellent graduation thesis award, at the same time, her graduation work "Welcome daily moon" was invited in Fresh Eyes 09: Falsification—6th Annual Exhibition of Dissertation Works in Painting from National Art Academies across China in He Xiangning Art Museum.

She began to observe life from multiple directions since 2010. Holding passion for life, she is a big fan of music and traveling. Music touches her soul while traveling helps enrich her experience. She shifted the focus on women themselves to a broader world. This explains why her works present a bright-colored world. Her passion for life can be found from her works like "Protagonist" (2011) showing jazz style, "Ring" (2011) showing a religious setting , "Boys" (2012) showing children floating among red colors (2012), showing a fanciful and rough picture of swans. The gorgeous black used in these works give a substantial proof.

"Attitude of Nature• 2012 Chinese Artist for wildlife Conservation Itinerant Exhibition " intrigued her very much. She had been actively involved in the African wildlife protection campaigns, seminars and tour of exhibitions, which benefited her a lot. She shifted her focus on wildlife protection this year. She headed to Tibet and reached HOh Xil Tibetan antelope natural reserve. She saw caged black bear at Linzhi. She also witnessed animals running freely on the open desert and plateau where no one lives. The coexistence between human beings and nature on one hand as well as human being and other species on the other plants a seed in her mind that encourages her to think about how mankind lives and how environment exerts both positive and negative influence on other species. She interpreted these perplexities with a series of works like "Loneliness appeal" (2012), "Liberty & romantic" (2012) "Pure land" (2013).

Her works are universally abstract, with budding of emotionalized colors and subconscious. She does not paint us stories. Her works convey intuitively her thinking and emotion. Perhaps, it is too early to find something wise or deep in her works. However, she will fight for that. At least, she holds her passion for life and holds on to what she wants her to be. By capturing the details of life, she fills the works with the passion for and thinking about life using her emotionalized colors.

Liu Zhehai Mar.2013 Chongqing University

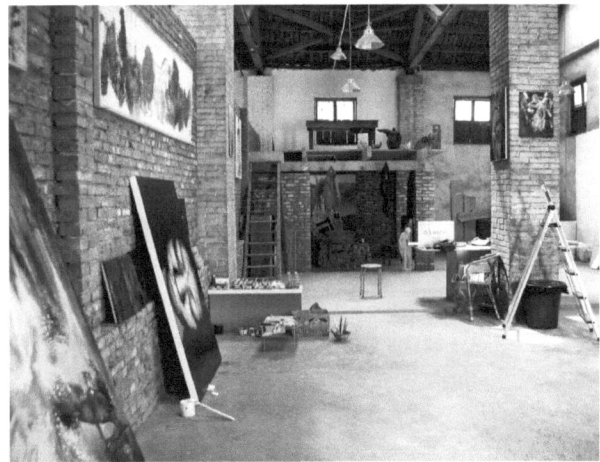

The Life Secret of Wu Shuang's Works

Written by Wang Xiaojian

Everyone faces a variety of temptations and choices in today's society. To put it this way, to persevere to the end is universally desired. However, to make it lies in personal capability and a good reason. This also happens to artists. An artist would like to go for art when art is more appealing than anything else. An artist would like to persevere to the end only when there is every reason to hold onto it rather than give it up. As a younger artist of such age under increasingly greater financial and mental stress, the harder Wu Shuang found it to move on, the more she needs a powerful reason to have a spiritual support.

The opening remark is apparently not in line with the title, and even can be seen as something off track. Such opening remark does not run off track with such a logic as "art lies in perseverance". As a matter of fact, several significant exhibitions held recently believed it. Let me say "One fellow's 3040 —— Wang Lin book fair". "Fair of works looking back Ma Yiping's 50 years of art education experience with his students and colleagues" " Wang Guangyi's retrospective exhibition", "Story in Guiyang" "Modern Route —— YuNan contemporary oil painting exhibition". All of these present stories about a fellow or a region as well as a fellow's or a region's perseverance. Compared to them and their stories, Wu Shuang just has a beginning. Compared to people of her age, she could be one of few artists that survived.

There is no need to talk about why she has survived from the prospective of art market. This is also true with interest and ideal which tend to be very fragile when confronting a brutal market. What allows us to look at reasonably is whether an artist is able to find an extension or a higher level in his or her creations. It is obvious she has found it. From the overall style, her works tend to be somewhat dark and gloomy, consisting of abstract settings and/or specific or obscure erratic symbols. Her works universally present moods portrayed in an obscure and abstract setting. The symbols serve as decode for the moods. To put it in another way, moods represent tone of language and symbols language itself. It is selective for interpreting a word with either a calm speech or a fierce roar. The following paragraph is an explanatory summary about her works, which also can be called self-revelation.

"With intuition, I have been looking at human's instinct needs and behavioral experience as they grow up. During my initial creation from 2008

to see them as a 'self-enlightening in art' . Meanwhile, I am trying to explore an expression of art language in a new sense. I made my debut , '······ Born' and my graduation work, 'Welcome daily moon' and others as well at that time."

I never quoted artists' own words in my critic articles since their words are not about criticizing. Criticism refers to critic's view of the works instead of artists' idea, let alone notes to artists' thoughts. The reason for such an exception results from a fact that critics are strongly requested to interpret works with popular language by art galleries that recently spring up and mass media that just began to be concerned about contemporary art. This is also to say, critics are asked to act as a mass-oriented interpreter. Hence, there was a dispute that took place at the 6th critic annual meeting for China's fine art held in Xi'an art gallery where Yang Chaoming, Xi'an art gallery curator, proposed such a hope. However, Pi Daojian, chairman on duty, explicitly remarked that it is hard to do so. Consequently, this essay keeps both popularity and its own artistic language at its best. It regrettably takes none care of the needs of illiterate.

Wu Shuang's works center around life, sex and female. Life as a theme in contemporary art comes from western life philosophy or also called non-rational philosophy. The representative thinkers include Sartre, Nietzsche, Freud and alike. "Those intense feelings sealed beneath subconscious" mentioned in her own words comes from Freud's study of subconscious. Freud separates a single life into id, ego and superego. "Ego" presents a socialized me who is subject to social norms under which a single person is humanized and has to conform to virtue and morality; "id" presents a me restrained by social norms and hidden from the public. To put it this way, "id" presents a person's animal nature or "the opposites against virtue and morality" . "id" is inherent in life. Freud called it libido. "Ego" is the representation of consciousness and "id" is that of subconscious.

The social norm on sex came first with all others built on it. Therefore, there is an increasingly fierce contradiction and conflict between the socialized "ego" and the instinct "id" . The works of literature displaying the contradiction and conflict have been universally around since ancient times. However, the representation varies by different cultures and historical periods. Freud's idea sprang up during a milestone of western changing from "agricultural to non-agricultural" status. The effect of his idea on China gets stronger as a milestone of changing from "agricultural to non-agricultural" status comes closer. Early in the changing period, both the west and China embraced freedom of marriage, with the west changing from aristocratic union by marriage to freedom of marriage as well as China changing from arranged marriage to freedom of marriage. The freedom in choosing a target for the realization of sexual instinct poses as a major problem rather than a person's own sexual instinct. In a society where an individual is deprived of his or her right to make a choice, he or she is forced to fix on one single target. In this case, making a choice can be explained to be obedience and resistance. Once freedom of choice is acquired, hesitation emerges. Consequently, sex instinct would lose its target, which subsequently forms both increasingly-serious physical and mental concerns that universally can be found in today's people.

The same issue varies from China to the west and man to woman. Freud's idea actually is an extension from humanism in Revival of Learning which does can be found in today's people.

The same issue varies from China to the west and man to woman. Freud's idea actually is an extension from humanism in Revival of Learning which does not exist in China. The western democracy and spirit of freedom conduct the least control over people (to get hand off things that do not need control and to legislate to control things that have got to be controlled). China's Unitarianism and absolutism takes its maximum control over people (to control to a degree that extends as it can). Almost in all cultures around the world, a woman's virginity is deemed as an extremely-severe moral norm exclusively set for women. Hence, whether she lives in an enlightened society or a backward one, a woman's life instinct is restrained to a higher extent unless she goes against morality by living as a whore. In this case, women can do nothing but wait. Otherwise, they would be condemned as a dirty woman. The reason why women prefer works of literature about love stories is to find a legal way to unleash their instinct needs. In addition, women also have to deal with their inherent fertility. Therefore, women are subject to more outstanding sexual and emotional issues under the same social conditions. For this, women usually find it difficult. In today's information-based world, the issue regarding Chinese women's sex and emotion tends to be more severe. We would see a clear route of thinking in Wu Shuang's works by having a clear understanding of the issues described above: today's Chinese women's identity (id) —— study from a woman's prospective (ego) —— emotional expression. The female emotion expressed through subconscious can be seen as a missing part of China's humanism.

I first gave an analysis into the theory on which her creations are based and now go to have a detailed study of the composition of her works. She has an in-depth and intimate vision. Her subjective emotion is perfectly integrated into the colors used in her works. It is usual to represent subconscious by using obscurity. This is also true with her works. Her works generally fall into 4 categories by the extent of obscurity: clear symbol, obscure symbol, random symbol and abstract representation.

1. Clear Symbol

Wu Shuang's works predominate in clear symbol so far. You find a woman in her works like "Rambo", "Phage in me", "Manjusaka", "Graceful", "More attractive than makeup"and "Protagonist". The woman in "Rambo" is covered on her face with mask-like make-up, and on her head and neck with gauze kerchief, and on her breast and private parts with black colors, leaving other parts exposed. Set in a flame-like pink canvas, she has been masculinized from her figure and akimbo posture. All of these show a woman's mental conflict between self-veiling and the desire to expose as well as an appeal to be feminized. Therefore, "Rambo" should be translated as going back to life instinct. "Manjusaka" and "Mandarava" represent "the flower on red shore" and "the flower on the white shore" respectively. The former has a richer moral. It is called "sad memory" in South Korea and called "Missing each other" in Japan. "Manjusaka" of her apparently refuses to illustrate the moral hidden in the two flowers. On the contrary, she titled the red flower as two flowers casually hit her mind for the burning red background and a woman's white dressing in a Broadway musical drama. As a result, what the audience had felt is unabashed feminine and physical desires instead of "sad memory" or "missing each other".

The woman in "Protagonist" wears a black coat, a black hat and a white glove on her left hand, with her right hand holding a bottle of wine and burning flame set behind her back. It is quite random in the connection between the picture and its title. From a far-fetched point of view, there is a connection between a woman's leading role in the western salon and the author's appeal to centralize a woman. Broadway music drama can also be found in the woman in "More attractive than makeup" . The black setting is glistening light of waves as if it was set in a dreamland. This presents a desire in a woman's subconscious to show her "id" . "Graceful" is a title that comes from a word, "You feel a beauty's charm as she looks back and smiles", which is quoted from Everlasting Regret written by Bai Juyi. The poem paid a tribute to a woman for whom the emperor is crazy. This work portrays only a woman's heterosexual expectation and predominant desire instead of alluring appearance. The woman in "Phage in me" is generally set in an emotional depression except her face. In combination with the burning flame released from the cigarette held in mouth, there is a strong formation of cause and consequence. Smoking, eating banana and licking cherry and others all are lip symbols to show signs of female life desires.

Both "Boys" and "Embarrassing stay" present us a picture of two boys travelling on the same boat. The boat is like either a rubber raft or a mattress. The setting looks like billow that is about to swallow them. The setting does not symbolize billowy desires when analyzing from the prospective of colors being used. On the contrary, it symbolizes them getting drowned in their ego desires or in their lust to which we can't find an answer. "Ring" portrays a papacy-like flaggy man who holds a rifle in his hand rather than a wand. Papacy represents faith, male authority and supreme ceremony. Rifle serves as a symbol of penis. Hence, the best explanation to the title is "firing gun" which is the synonym for "having sex" . Meanwhile, the supreme ceremony that associates with "firing gun" must be wedding party. There is only a rabbit in "Stupid rabbit" which represents baby and delivery in Wu Shuang's symbol system.

"Wildlife" features a dull black bird painted in an explosive color setting in it. "Monologist" features a dog-like animal painted in an out-of-order setting in colors of red, green and black. The red lip interacts with the red emerging from a dissipated setting. Mouth is a symbol of desire. It shows a higher level of desire when it turns red. This happens to align with red in a psychological sense. The works of this type should be explained as animals with restrained or vanished savagery. The humanized animalism represents the restrain and destroys of life instinct. The comparison between a crouching cattle and a woman's shadow can be identified from the emotionalized-color picture of "Pure land" . Cattle is a tamed animal and features mildness, toughness and diligence all of which can be compared to a woman's current status. However, the emotionalized colors reflect energy that waits to be released.

Based on the study made above, it is found that her works of clear symbol are only visually clear and linguistically quite obscure. Such obscurity results from a random selection of title to a large extent.

2. Obscure Symbol

"Power of a girl" sketches a bent woman grabbing a sickle. Wearing high heels, she has a hairstyle shaped like two sickles. A woman's dressing tends to be far more complicated than that of man while wearing high heels gives less pain than foot-binding. The sketch undoubtedly reflects an inequality, extra troubles and pains for workingwomen. However, a woman's charm tends to be discounted without those dressings. That is also to say, this is the only way to keep a woman's power. "Each party" shows two opposite fellows. They are visually obscure. They are sexually opposite for the characteristics reflected from their arms. The crazy style of drawing exactly suggests their craze for each other. "Memory of the sea", "Walk" and "Go home" were works of the same period. They seemingly portray young boys and girls. But the obscurity lies in their face and sexual features. This is true of the visual characteristics in an artist's memory. However, "Walk" and "Go home" gives an emphasis to the innocence and purity found in young boys and girls. The title reasonably suggests it is about the status that special group of people (e.g. children or teenagers suffering autistic disorder) fall in, the contradiction between care and pain, impulse and patience, intimacy and loneliness. "Temptation" features a recumbent female figure burning with lust and a black cat next to her. Woman + cat = family + absence of man. It arguably expresses an idea, "The only company with me is my cat". The lengthened and thickened cat tail turns into a bald white and gets bent to point to the woman, which exactly reflects a woman's burning expectation.

"Let's grow up together , my darling woman" is a photography work did by Wu Shuang. It is like a behavior shooting. There are several profiles bound with ropes, which are sexually obscure or more like man. But binding would also dilute a woman's physical features. The binding onto the body definitely represents the constraint applied to people. Whether you are a man or a woman, you grow up with constraints in the real world, with sexual constraint coming first. "Running trees" features a sexually-obscure profile in its center and a section of green trunk where viscera-like things reach out of some black holes. Bloodstain and eyes seem to be found on the small green trunk at the right and lower corner of the picture. In combination with a weird title, this picture reflects pieces of dream and blank anxieties in association with gestation.

The profiles that tend to be feminized can be found in works like "Breathe", "Maid" , "Perplexed" , "Shallow drowning" and others. It is hard to identify, especially with "Perplexity" which is obscure to an extent that it almost can not be identified. "⋯ ⋯ Born" , "please forgive me" "Kids" , "Hurt" and "Cry" are works of the same series, all about pregnant woman. "⋯⋯born" portrays a black figure pregnant with a bunch of rabbits and little monsters. "Hurt" seems to portray a female figure which has been through delivery or abortion and holds a visually-obscure rabbit. "Cry" features a female figure pregnant with a rabbit visually-obscure rabbit. "Cry" features a female figure pregnant with a rabbit with several other rabbits fancifully floating around. These visually-obscure symbols and obscure pictures are closer to dream, basically talking about female or sex in physical sense.

3. Random Symbol

"Revel" features a hip and a running man, which arguably shows a carnival relationship between man and woman. It is not so much about being a running man as being a randomly-added image. The title is quite random too. "Welcome daily moon" features a pregnant female figure, a private part and a female figure with a hollow abdomen as well as death's-head, skeletons of infants, birds and beasts, the moon and an arm reaching out to the moon. Except some kraurotic branches and an unidentifiable setting sun, all other objects can not be identified in "Sunset" . Much effort must be paid to find out the boys in "A lose child" . This provokes the idea of embryo or abortion. "Dancing shoes" features a pair of identifiable feet from a female figure. "The lonely appeal" features some branches and sexually-seductive hair. You might find it harder to interpret works like "Liberty & romance" , "Perfect irregularities" , "Upsurge" , "Phoenix" and others. They all consist of a combination of emotionalized colors and some perplexing or vague life symbols.

4. Abstract Representation

Abstract representation are represented by "Fox's love" , "Sea horse" , "Lady" , "Memory of whirlpool" , "Movement" , "Dream" and others. They all are simple reflection of a combination of emotionalized colors. And, these emotions are special parts of woman, like expectation, irritation, anxiety, being excited, depression unleashing and so on. Works of this type is highly appreciable and readable. This is also a characteristic of abstract art and a little bit like music. Furthermore, abstract art is exactly linked to music. Both abstract art and music do not entail wordy expression, which is their similarity. However, words serve as the basic unit of linguistic meaning. The only thing that is readable is the title of her abstract works. Like those of other works, the titles are not informative for the picture and even can be considered as a random choice. To be exact, they represent a randomness dancing with an emotion that is true of the picture. All titles and pictures are like dance partners in a ball.

Randomness and accidental predominate in her works which reveal an artist's impulse from his or her subconscious. The revelation comes naturally as life instinct has been constantly shielded and depressed by consciousness. Even though artists tend to have a clear mind and to be controlled by consciousness during their creation, they would unwittingly try to dilute their consciousness as soon as possible and approach subconscious as randomness and accidental occur again and again. To be exact, artists sense and recognize the depression from their subconscious and try to express such depression unwittingly.

Traditional art usually gets round sex by advertising "love" and tries to cover the inner craze under an aesthetic appearance. However, modern art goes in an opposite direction by seeing life impulse as decent appeal and expression. As a female artist, Wu Shuang takes her gut to unleash the physical and mental reaction caused by ovum, including love, lust, and pregnancy and as far as some ultimate topics like life and death. Ovum is free of idea and moral constraint. It is born to expect sperm' s arrival. It conveys the expectation throughout the body and turns its short life cycle into a woman's proper appeal.

Is ovum a devil? No, God makes it. Is it wrong for ovum to expect sperm' s arrival? No, it is a property granted by God. Is it wrong for ovum to convey its birth and expectation to its owner in its own way? No, this is the right granted by God. A woman' s love is to carry out ovum' s target, "seeking its owner" . On behalf of ovum, she waits for sperm' s coming. I am not a woman. So, I cannot experience what ovum speaks to the body. But I believe that it has powerful life energy like a tree breaking through a stone. Wu Shuang just transforms such energy into her art —— listening to ovum's speech about art.

The final comment is about a fact that unlike most female artists, Wu Shuang admits she is a female artist. However, she does not go to the extreme by having an intention to overthrow patriarchy. She indeed is a post- feminism advocator, acknowledging the physical and mental difference between men and women. This probably has something to do with her character as a Chongqing spicy girl. As Chongqing girls have been traditionally moving somewhere else to live a new life, they tend to not hold a thought of "Women inferior to men" . She is of such an intellectual woman. In personality, she is supposed to be such "spicy girl" . She gives continuous charm to her works with such a character and boldly talks about the life secret of art.

Jan.7th, 2013 Huang Jueping

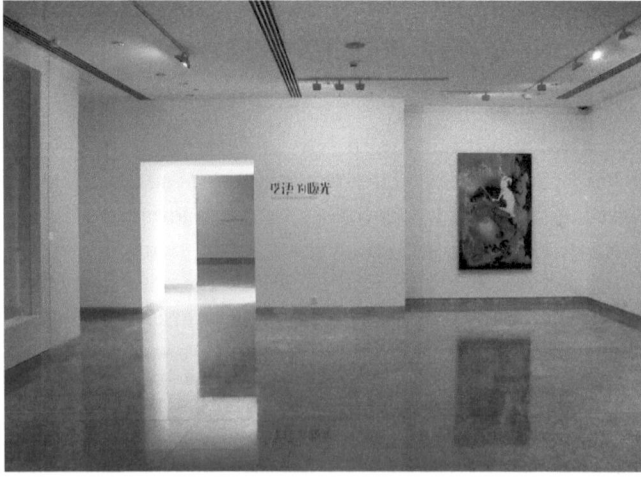

Art as her Nirvana
Written by Liang Yuan

Art and woman are born to stand against each other like two magnetic fields. Art keeps female as her company since its birth. Female can be involved in the painting only when they take their cloth off and become the representation. Such biased and brutal phenomenon has been around for a long time. Whereas, it is also very brutal for a female artist to create works with her personal experience and attempts to prize up the closed door. This feels like a female artist cuts bloodily her inside open to the public. Although pains and torture are paved on the way to the creation, both female and art do not seem to get rid of the suffering situation. The touching and cliff-hanging works like Xiangjing's sculpture, Tracey Emin's tent and Frida Kahol's self-portrait all are the results of female artists' personal experience and iterative reflection. They thought about life, death, love, hatred, pregnancy, sadness, pains, pleasure and others that exist in maternal world. They sacrificed their soul to the art, leaving a sere body moving on to seek experience and to be released again. This resembles the transformation into butterfly which takes continuous efforts to reach Nirvana. All the experience-based female artists are heroine.

The reason why I crown Wu Shuang, a female artist born after 1985s, a heroine not only lies in her courage to sail on her journey alone and to wholeheartedly go on a narrow path to be a female artist but also her being an experience-based female artist. She gets her inspiration and impetus from her personal experience and life stories. The themes in her works penetrate the presentation to find a link to affections and life. She interlaces continuously themes in her bold and innovative works, such as autobiography, fact, makeup, personal gains and loss, sadness and pleasure, meditation and confrontation as well as others. She records the past that involves passion and depression, thirst and torture, fantasy and suspicion, intoxication and hurt with such symbolic signs as glorious lady-boys on the stage, boys trembling in wind and waves, trees running with people, babies crouching in the uterus. She uses creation material as a "mental filter" to realize a self-deliverance and self-cognition. Her works are extremely inflammatory and contagious since she is able to have a cunning and direct fusion of themes and forms of works and to paint a great diversity of "autobiography"whenever she hits upon a feeling.

Mar. 2012　Chongqing

Art as Experience
Written by Yu Hansheng

Born into a family of scholars, Wu Shuang has a typical family of intellectuals. Her parents and grandparents all are professors with famous universities. Her grandpa is a very accomplished traditional Chinese painting artist. Influenced by her family, she enrolled in Chongqing cultural palace for the study of watercolor, calligraphy as well as the training and enlightenment education on art when she was only 6 years old. From then on, art became part of her childhood. Her lif e has always been tied to painting from her enrolling in interest-oriented class as a little girl, to learning Japanese cartoon and to become a professional artist now. Art has always been inseparable from her life. Her works vary from the early pregnancy series to the latest animal series. We see multiple techniques being used in those works, such as representation, abstract, super realism and others. Whichever technique she might use, there is always a constant theme, which is the constant concern about humanity, life and inner experience as well.

Traveling, a source of artistic inspiration

She is a big fan of traveling. Traveling and creation predominate in her life. She embarked on her journey through many countries in both Europe and Asia during her middle school years. She is undoubtedly dubbed a traveling lover. As for her, traveling is not only part of her but also part of her artistic creation. Her artistic inspiration is fueled from the places she has been to and the customs, culture, beautiful views she saw and met. She got her inspiration for "Final gorgeous bloom" series, her recent works from Thailand's lady-boys performance.

Her works feature bold and pretty colors, which are the results of inspiration from what, she saw and felt during her journey. As Zhuang Caoyun, a painter from Tang Dynasty, remarked, "Wai shi zao hua, zhong de xin yuan" , in which "zao hua" means natural views and "xin yuan" means artist' s inner understanding. The remark means artistic creation comes from a combination of inspiration from nature and the artist' s inner mind. Although the remark represents a creation theory for traditional Chinese painting, she gave an authentic comment to the remark with her "painting-on-journey" theory. A fellow who keeps his nose clean tends to get a happy life easier. However, a fellow who likes traveling adds more colors to his or her life. A traveling lover tends to be perceptual and is prone to focusing on spiritual freedom. Being reluctant to be restrained, prone to focusing on spiritual freedom. Being reluctant to be restrained, she would like to get her hands on new things, to meet new friends and take interests in strange and mysterious matters. This proves why she keeps a relatively constant theme through her works that vary in styles.

Life and experience

Life and experience walk through her works. Her obsession with "Life" can be found in her early works. She painted a series of works about gestation and pregnancy at the time. Life originates from gestation, a premise that allows human being to continue their gene one generation after another. Meanwhile, it is woman who predominates through the gestation. Consequently, gestation features a collective experience and a complex that only woman has. For a woman, gestation becomes an integral part of herself since she realizes what her sex sets her apart from a man. Exactly like boys playing fight-themed video games in their childhood, girls tend to prefer acting as some family members, such as a mother. This is a complex she is born to have. There are some works featuring this period, such as "Welcome daily moon" , "……Born" and others. As her graduation work, "Welcome daily moon" portrays an open scene of shining forever like the sun and the moon with her highly expressive techniques. The work features a group of women capable to give birth, with almost nothing on their faces but a profile. However, she was focused on the portrait of the intumescent belly and the fetuses that crouch inside the belly. Face serves as a window to identify an individual. Consequently, these rough images tend to become a symbol that represents people of the same kind. The women in this work exist as a common image instead of an individual with special attributes. Therefore, what the picture portrays represents a female collective experience infused with an artist's personal affections that involve the pain, happiness, fears and fantasy from gestation.

Final gorgeous bloom

Final gorgeous bloom is referred to as last blossom, the most beautiful and brilliant moment. Just like how her works portray the dancers when they blossom on the stage. In her readme, she believes performing artists are having a real self-release just when they are on the stage. "Stage is why I am here, I have no idea about what to do next when off the stage with all spotlights gone " said Lady Gaga interviewed by "Rolling Stone" magazine. We are taught by inertial thinking that the roles on the stage all are fake ones, and they are something created by people and even the properties are fake too. However, you can find a real you in the real life only. It may not be true if we take another look at it. Perhaps, the ones who would love to devote all they have to something they really want can find the best moments and their nature on the stage. However, the dancers feel embarrassed and are marginalized, and there are a few of them in the real life. They are misaligned both mentally and physically. The social moral norms ask them to go away from what their inner desires ask them to go to. There is no point talking about the authenticity in life when one's inner mind misaligns with his or her real life. So, the definition of authenticity and falsehood are no longer based on inertial thinking.

Final gorgeous bloom represents the end of spring. Just like a lot (a lot drawn by Sheyue, a role from novel called 'A Dream of Red Mansions') says "as flowers are blooming, the end of spring is on the way with other flowers to fade away." Consequently, Final gorgeous bloom also serves as a border between rising and falling. Brilliance is always followed by deterioration.

Conclusion

Sometimes, an artist's job feels like offering up a sacrifice that is exactly he or herself. An artist expresses honestly his or her experience without deliberate concealment and manic emotion. Personalized emotions give birth to the attributes that are presented collectively, allowing them to become resonant emotions. This is exactly what her works are about. Like she said "I would rather like to redesign my rough memory and experience subjectively than to present the reality as it is."

Aug. 2012 Chongqing

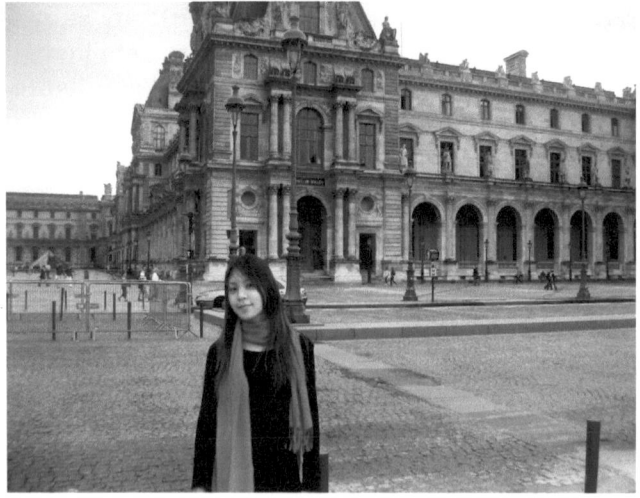

Shallow Dronwing Oil on Canvas 59" × 47.2" 2009

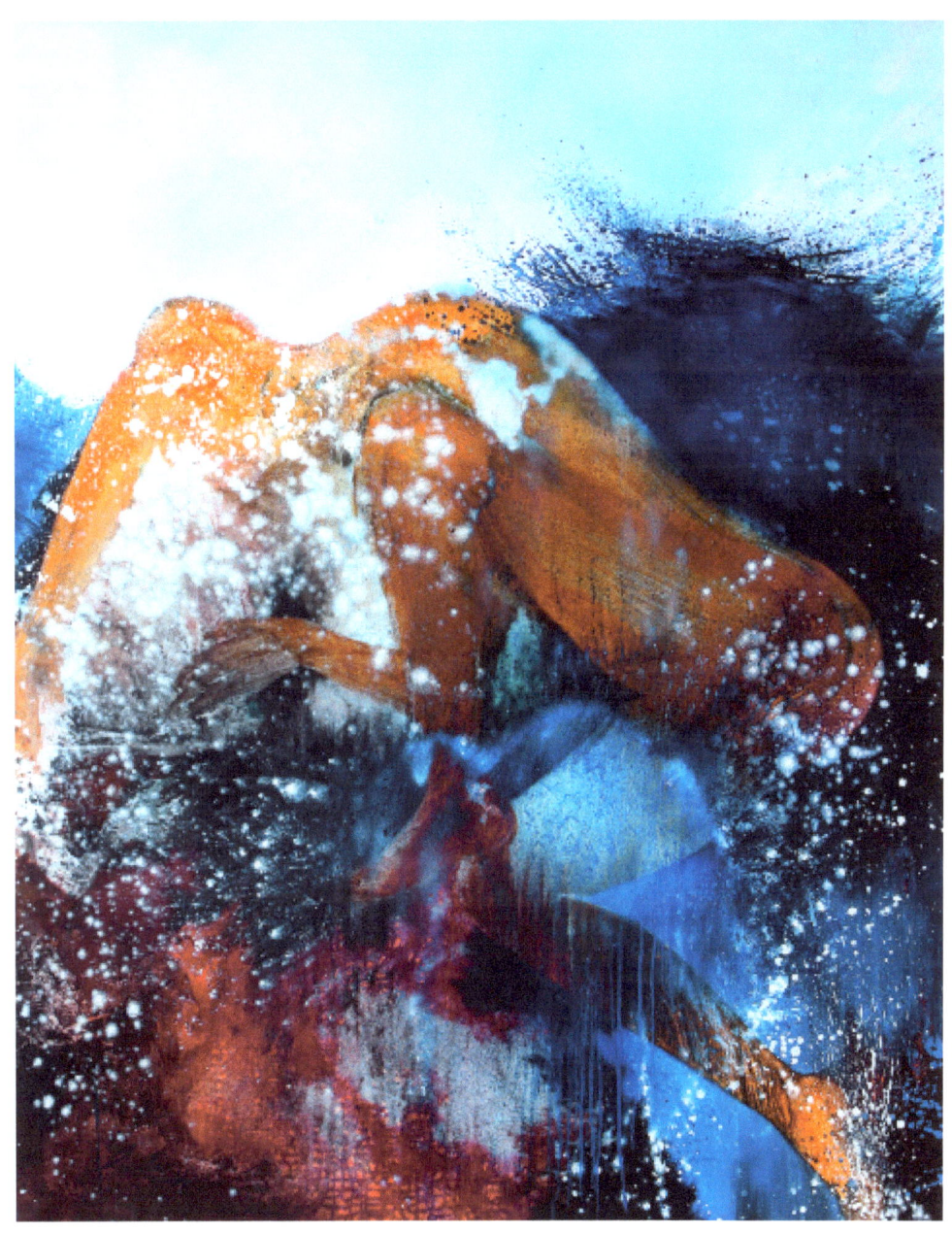

Monologist Oil on Canvas 31.5 " ϕ 2013

Phage in Me Oil on Canvas 31.5" × 47.2" 2013

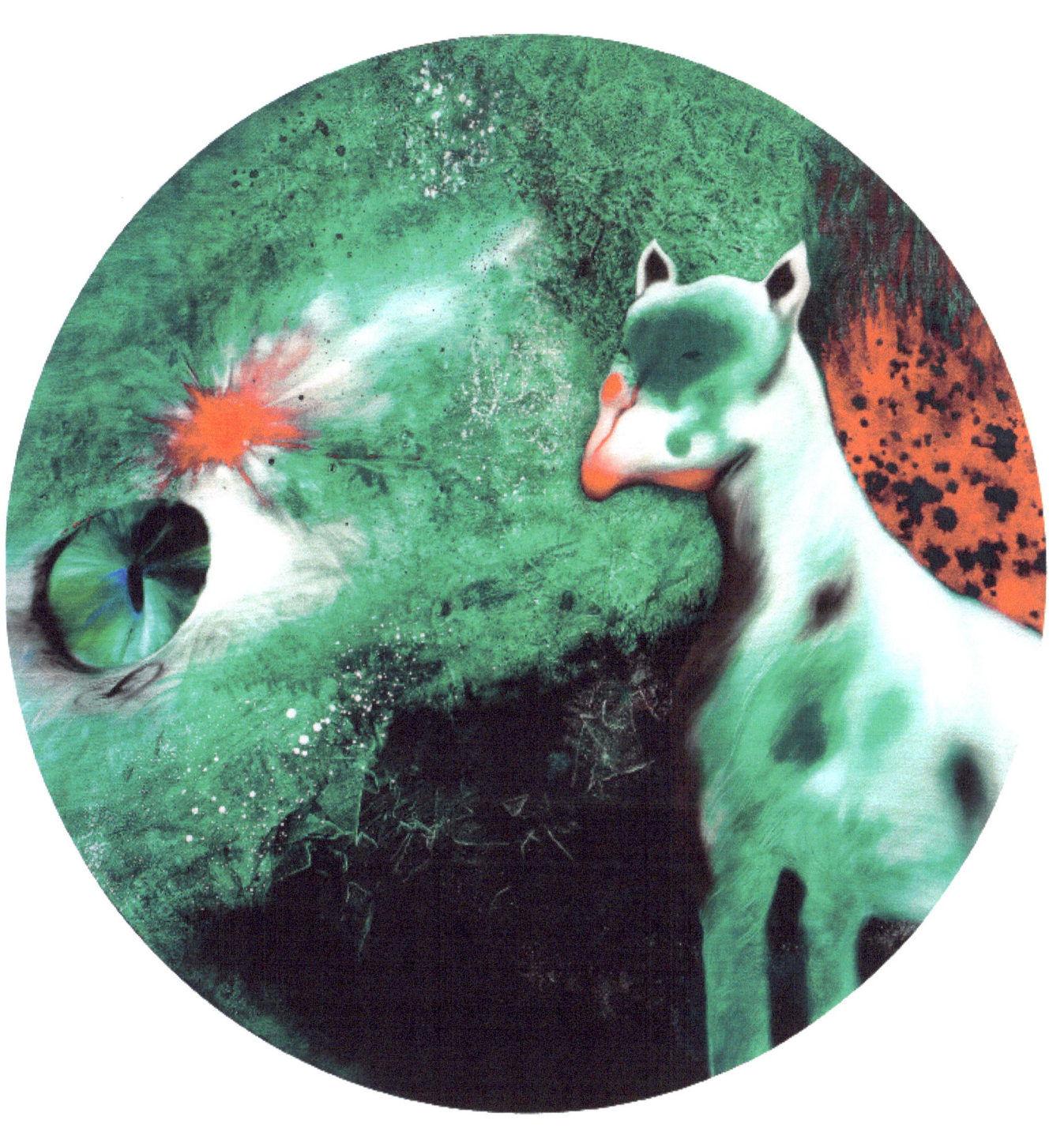

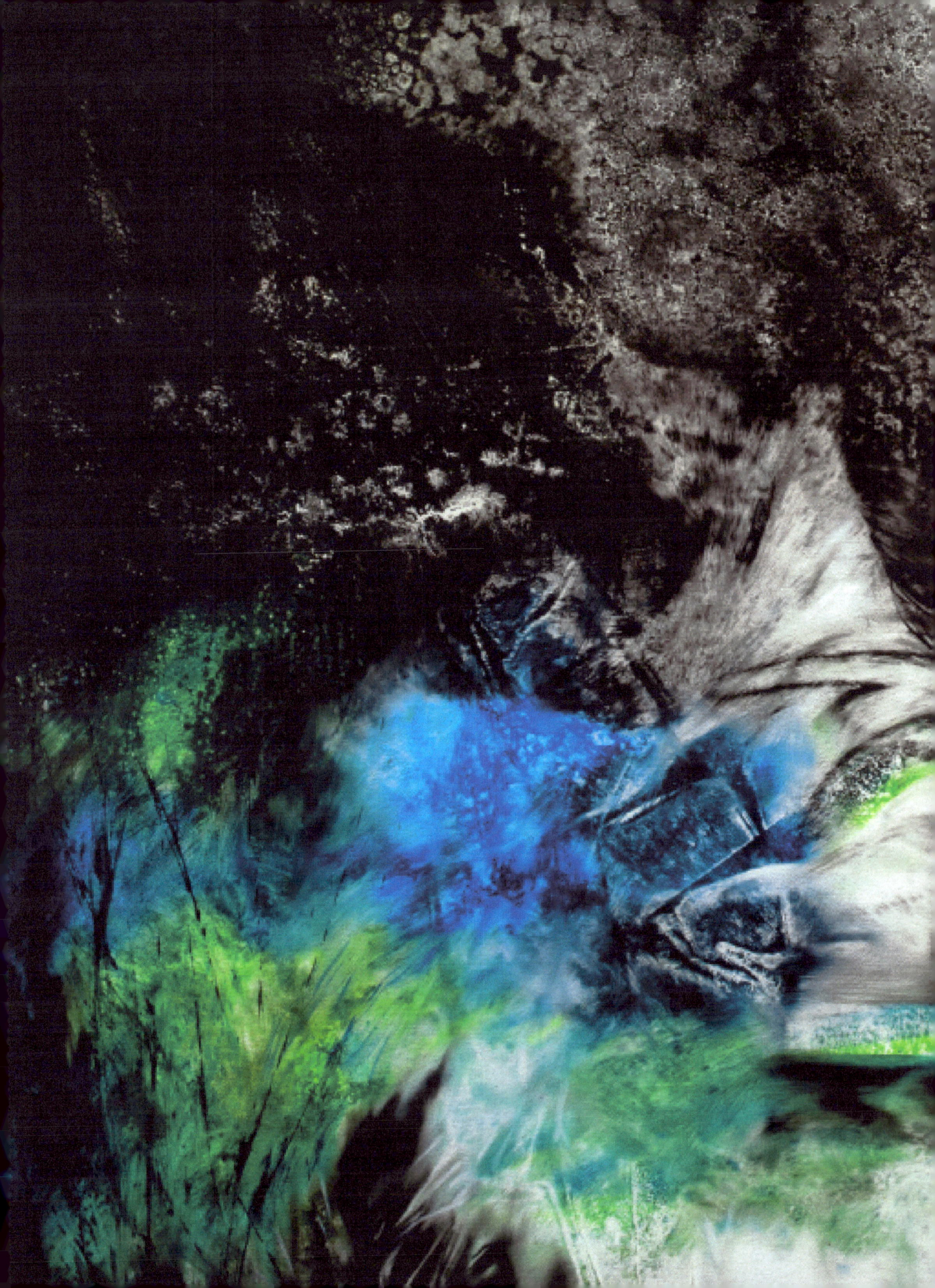

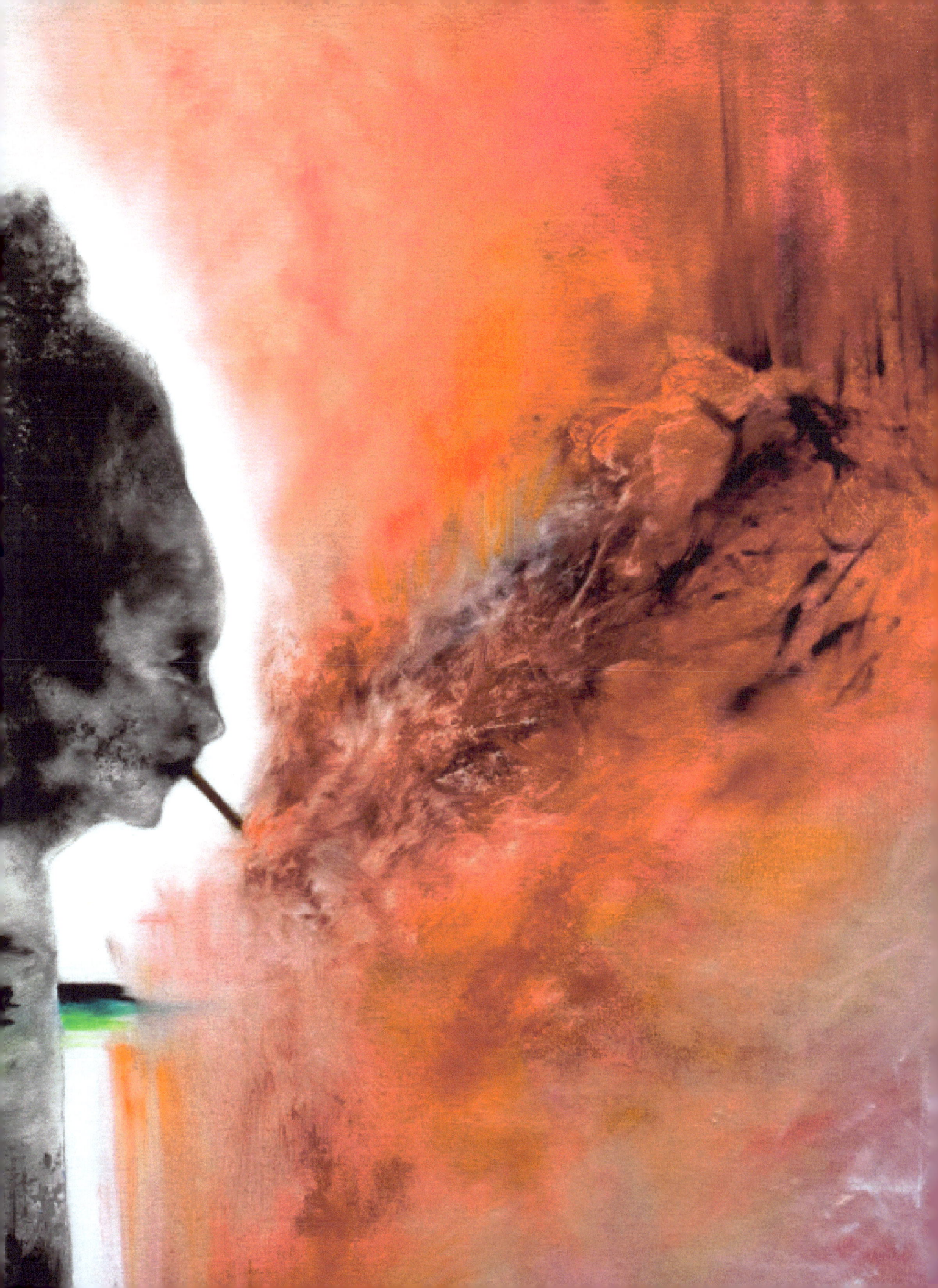

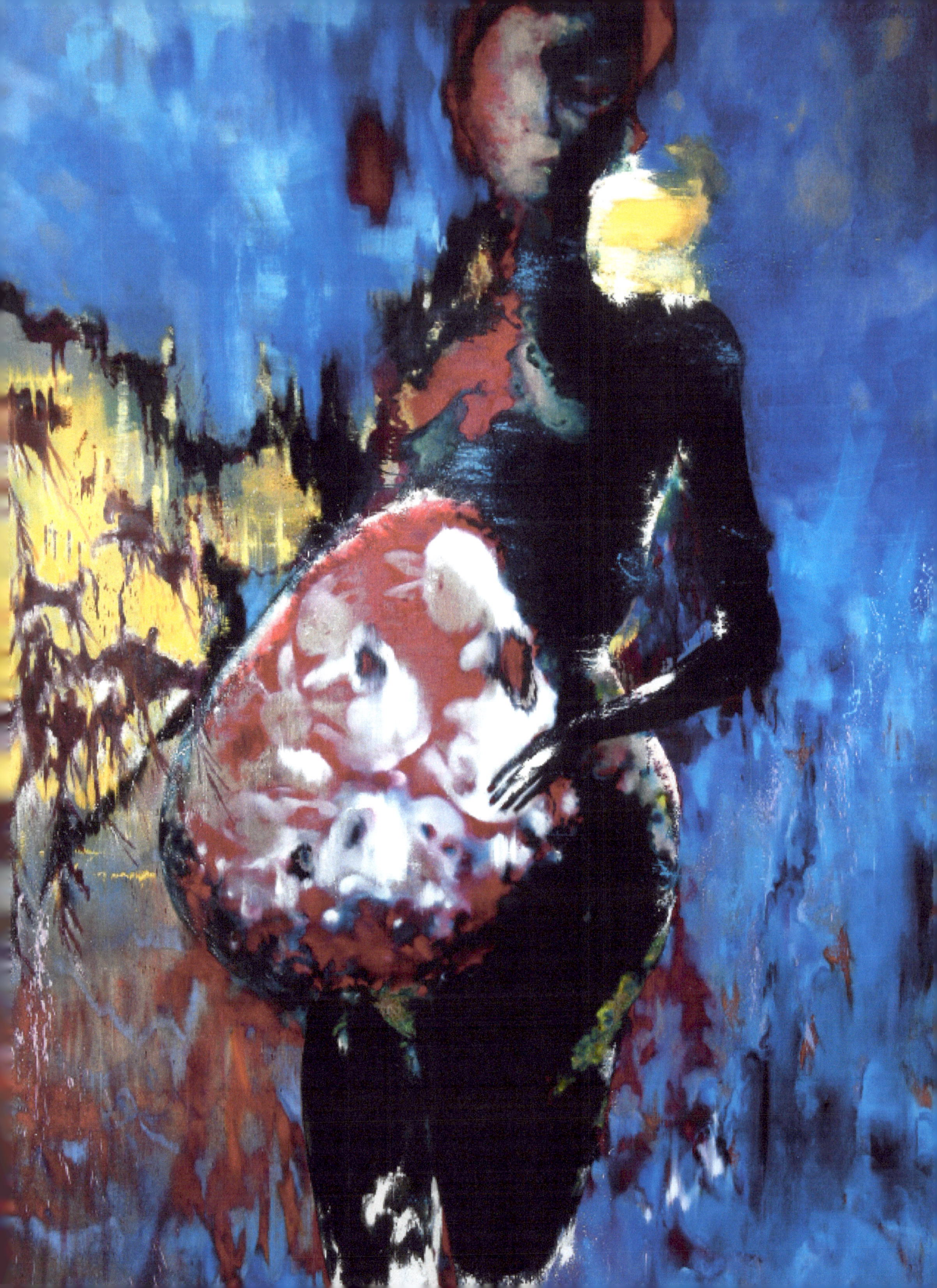

......Born Oil on Canvas 102.3" × 78.7" 2008

Welcome Daily Moon Oil on Canvas 78.7" × 196.9" 2009

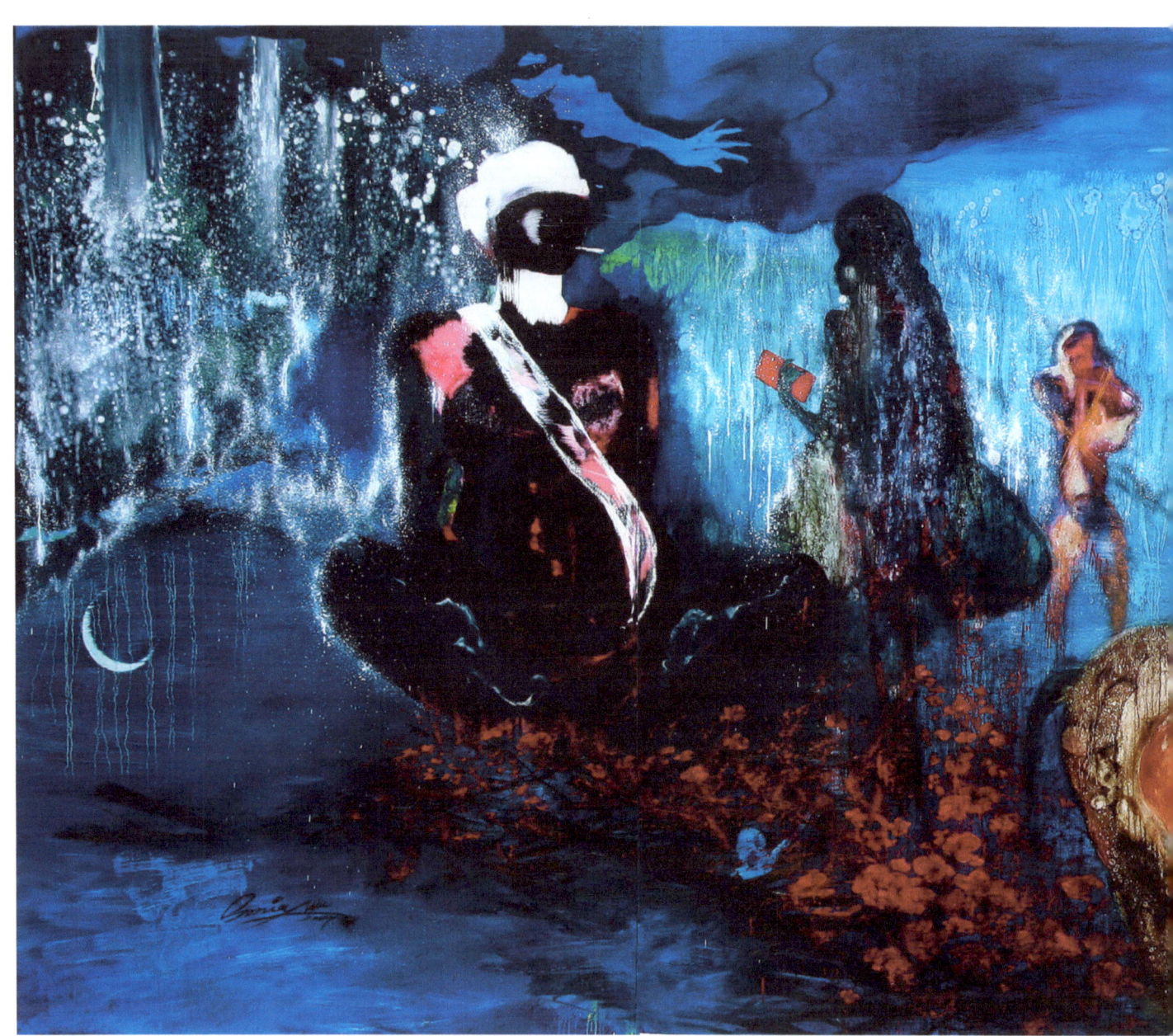

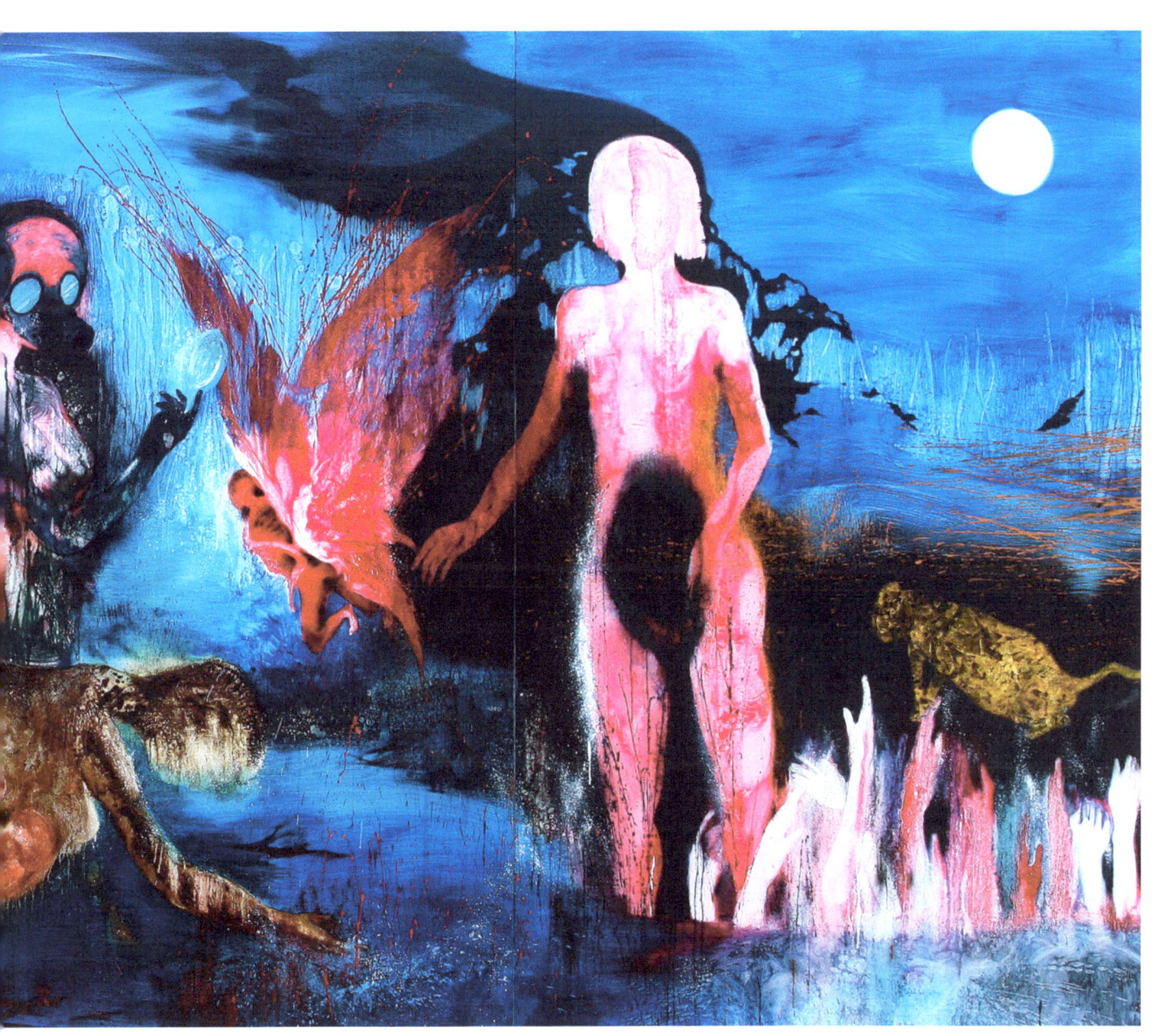

Power of a Girl Oil on Canvas 35.4" × 35.4" 2009

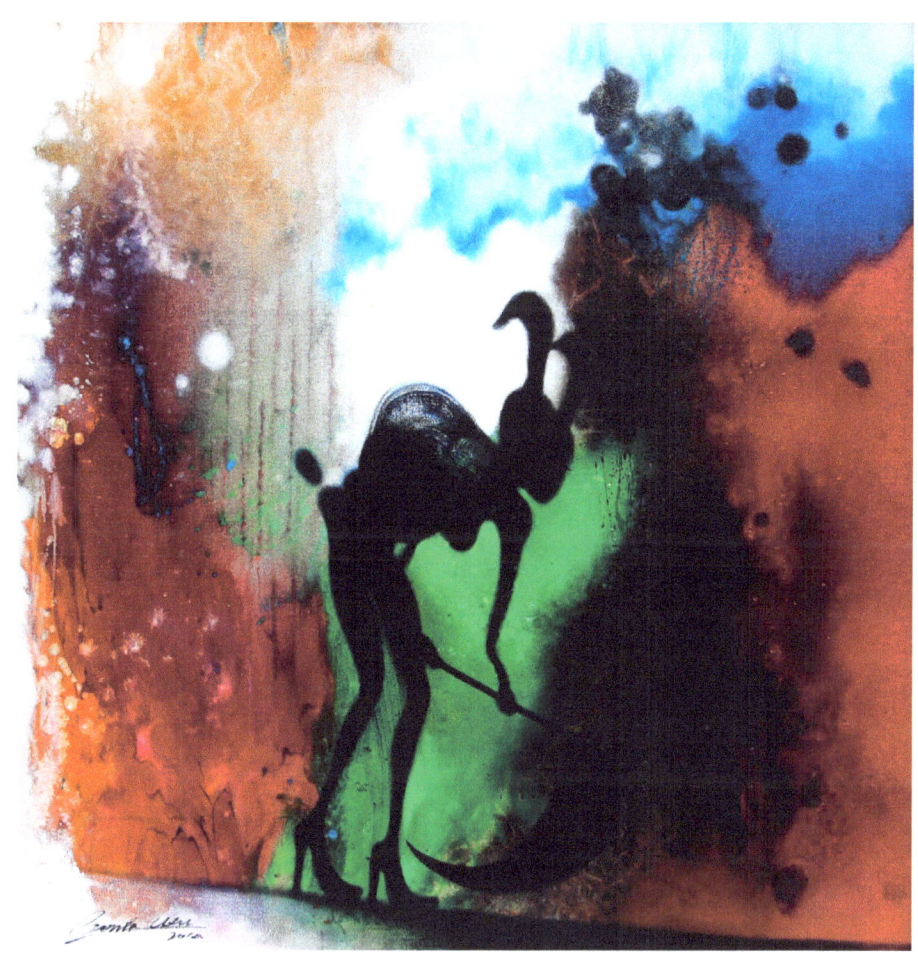

Softly Protest Oil on Canvas 70.9" × 47.2" 2009

Revel Oil on Canvas 55.1" × 78.7" 2011

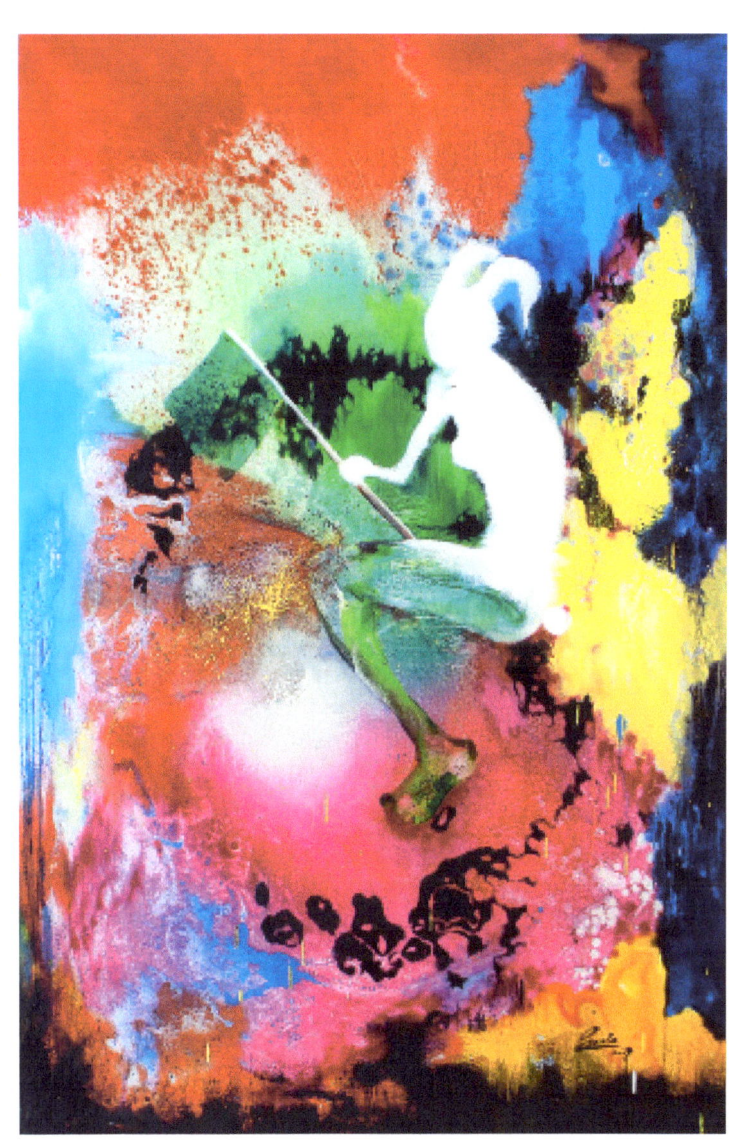

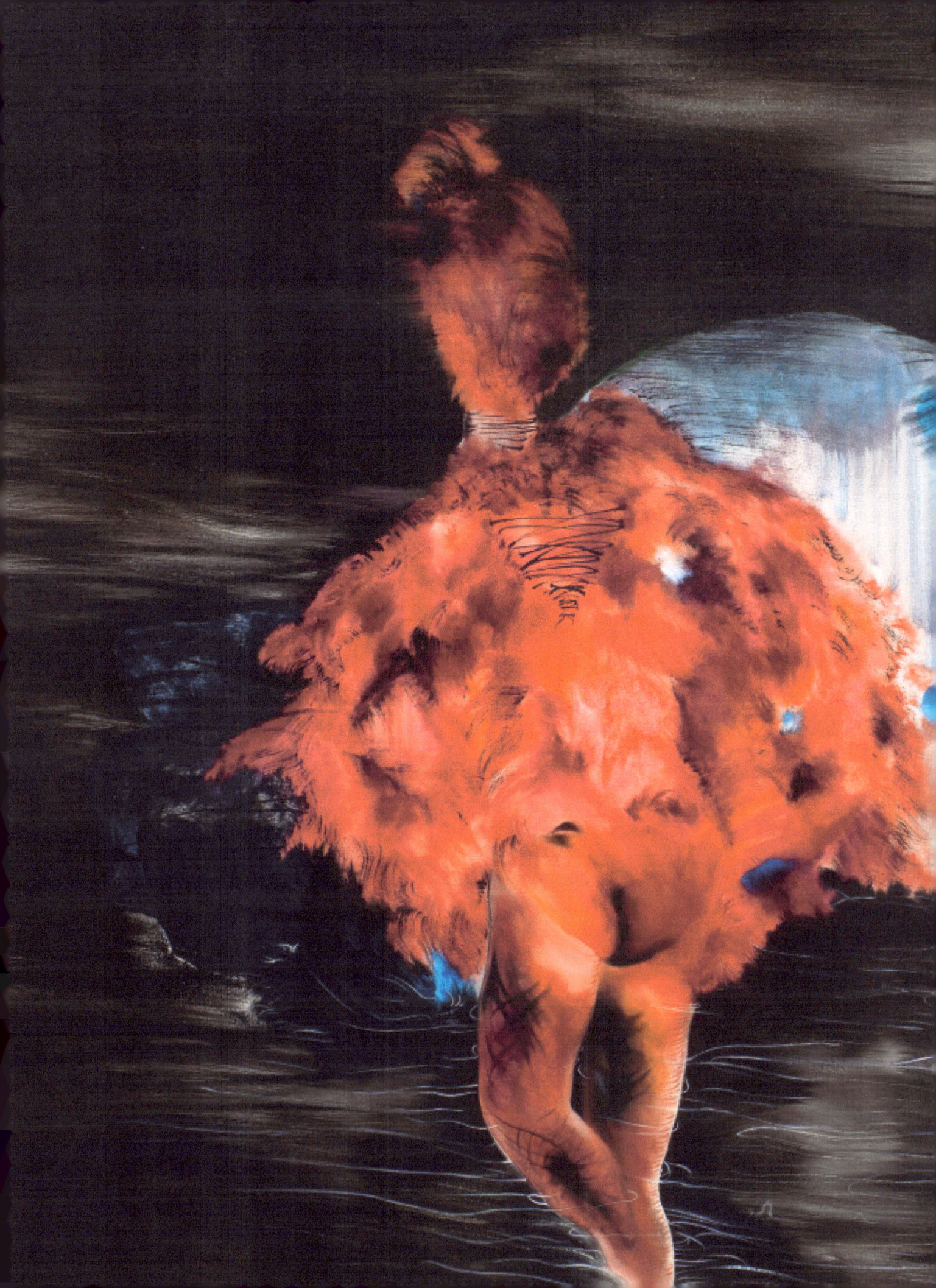

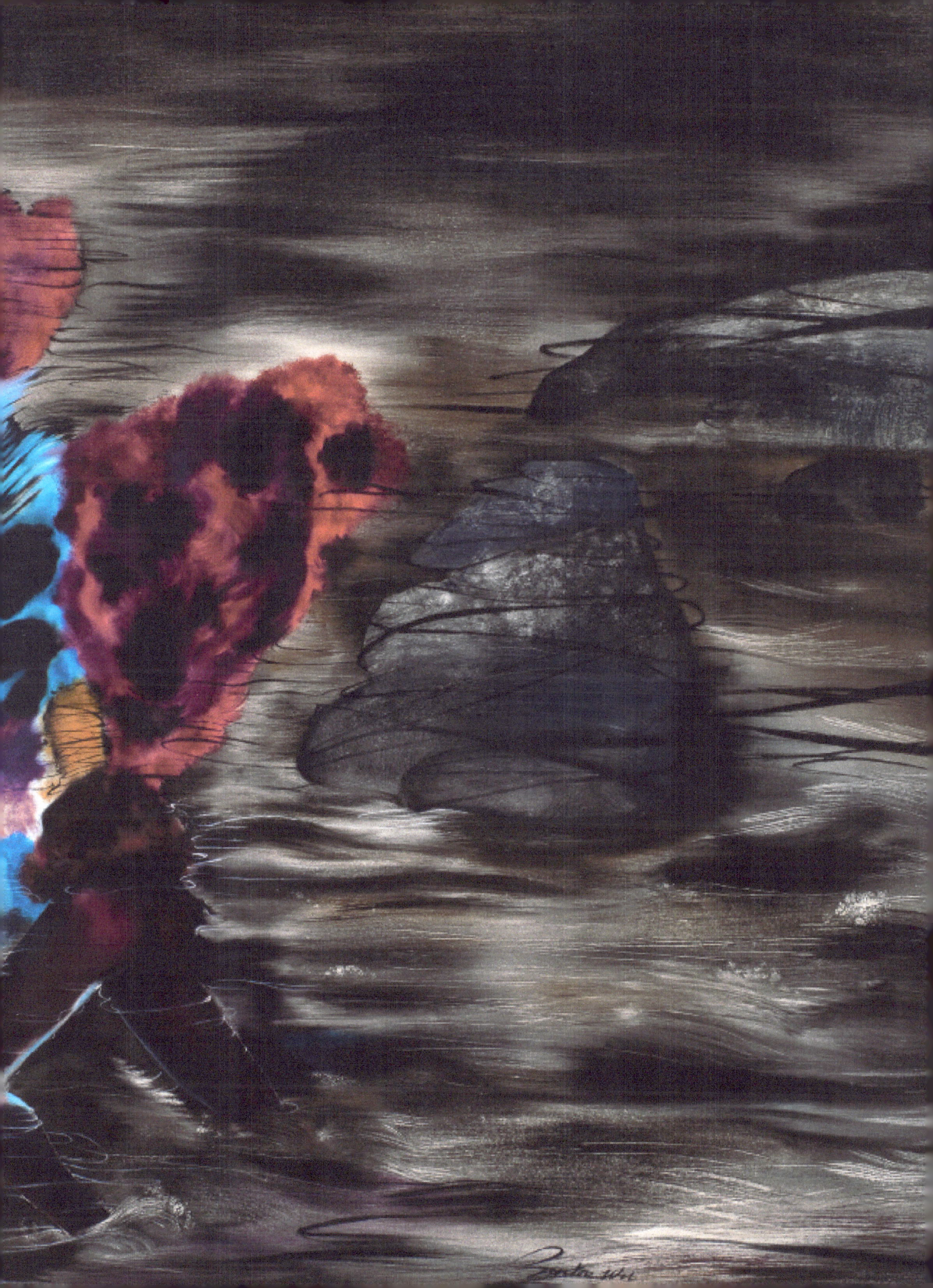

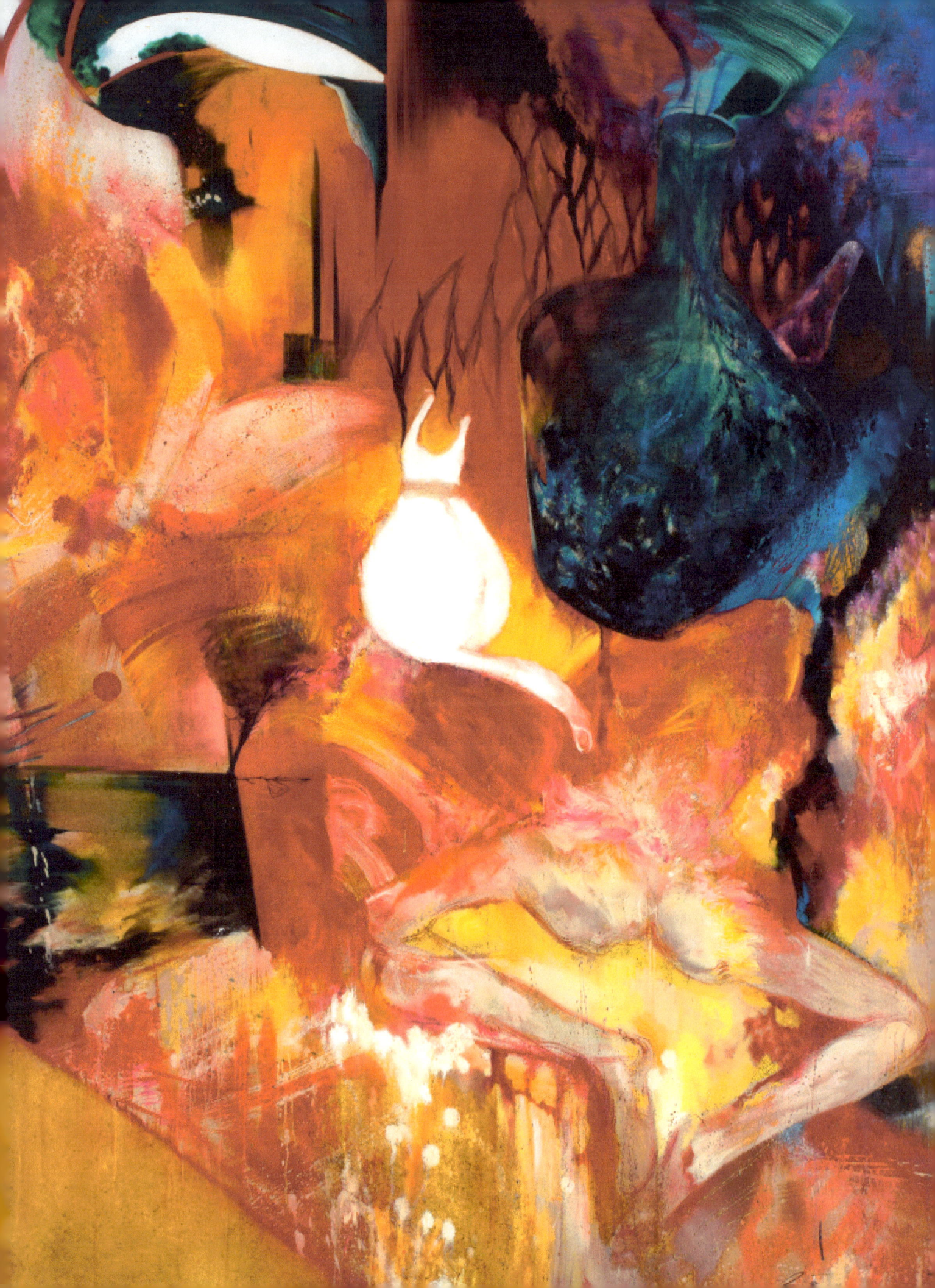

Upsurge Oil on Canvas   102.3 " × 78.7 "   2010

Primal Desire Oil on Canvas 39.4" × 39.4" 2010

Protagonist Oil on Canvas 59" × 78.7" 2011

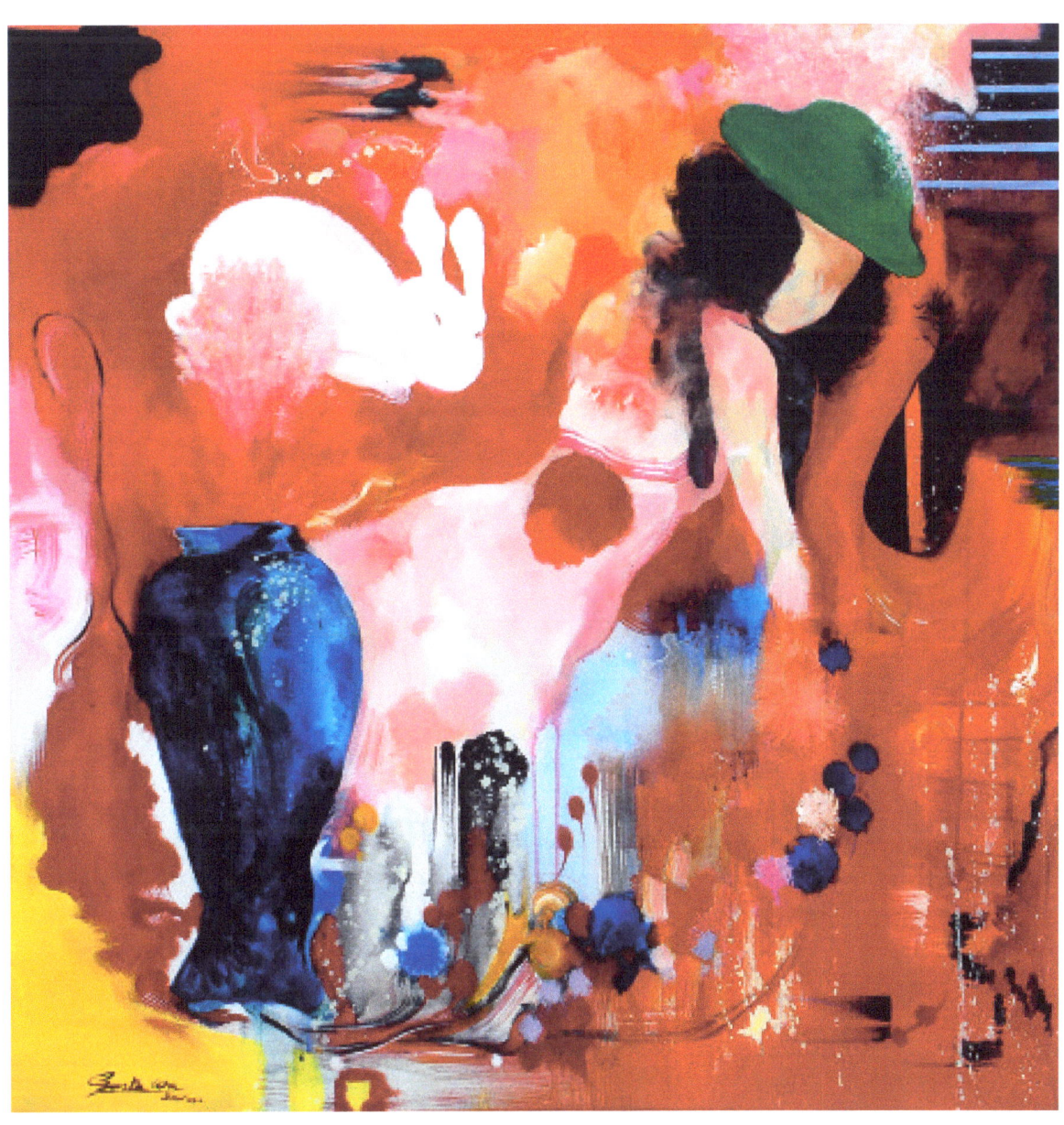

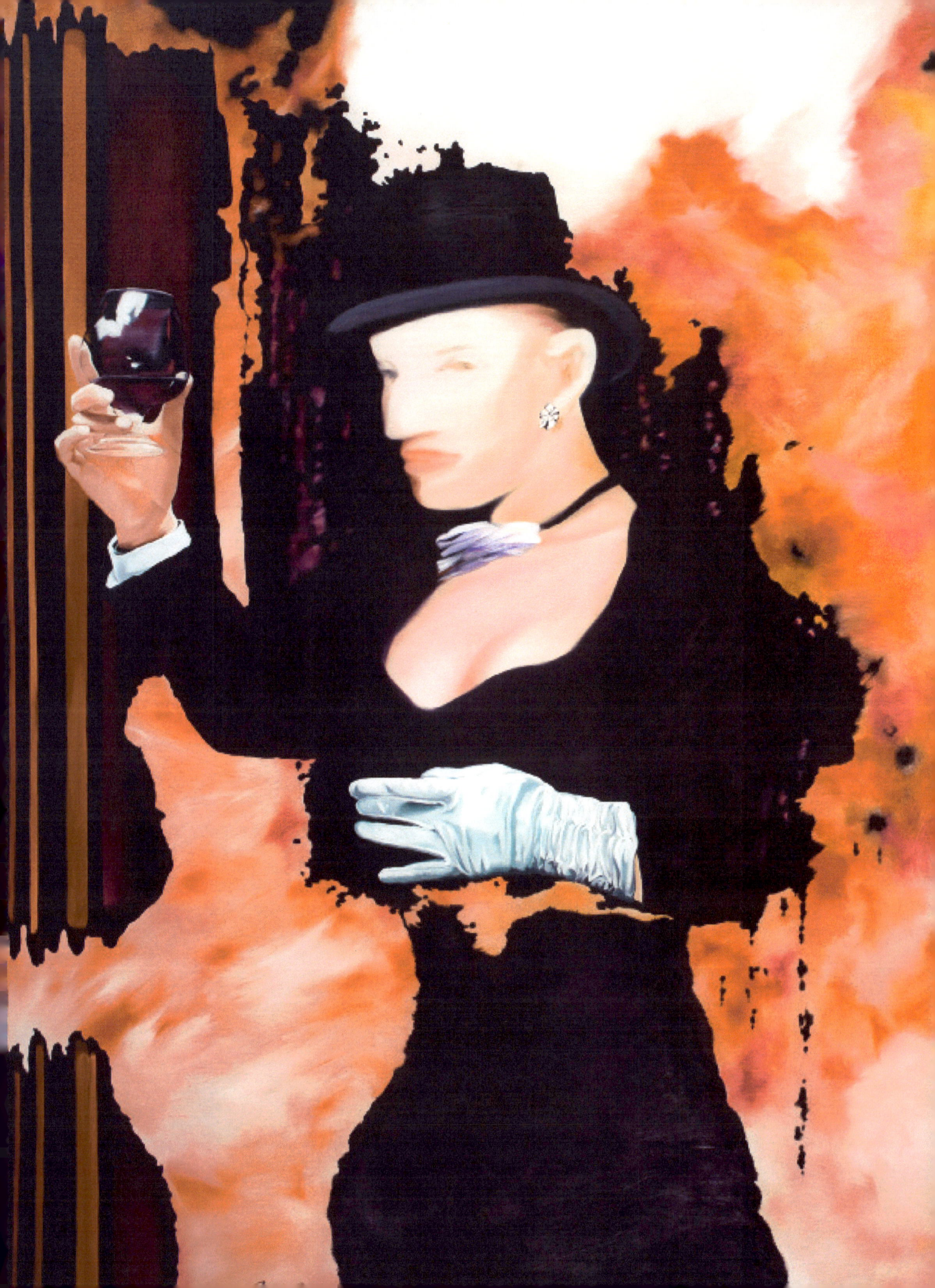

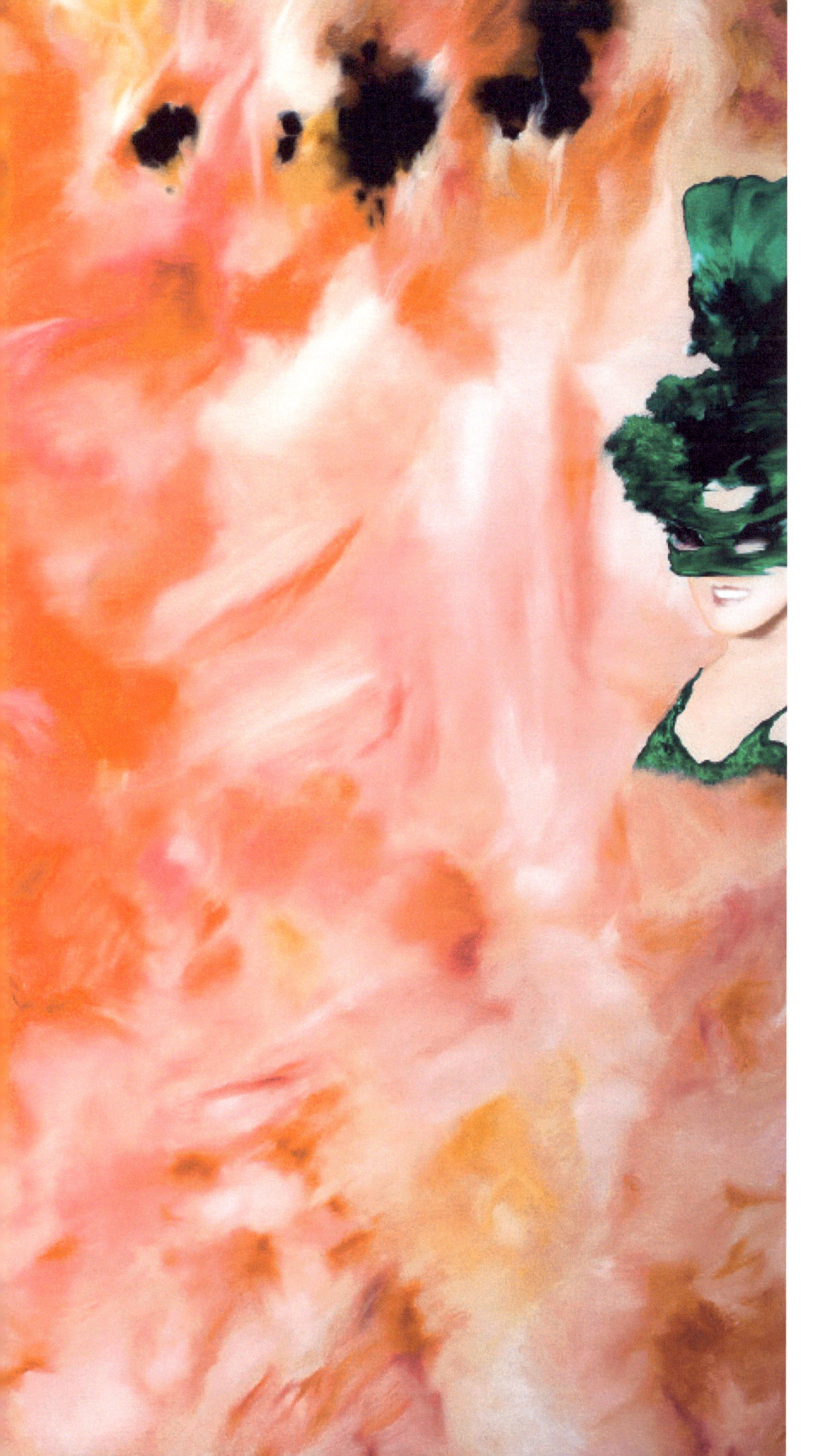

Phoenix Oil on Canvas   59" × 47.2" 2010

Ring Oil on Canvas 59"   × 78.7" 2011

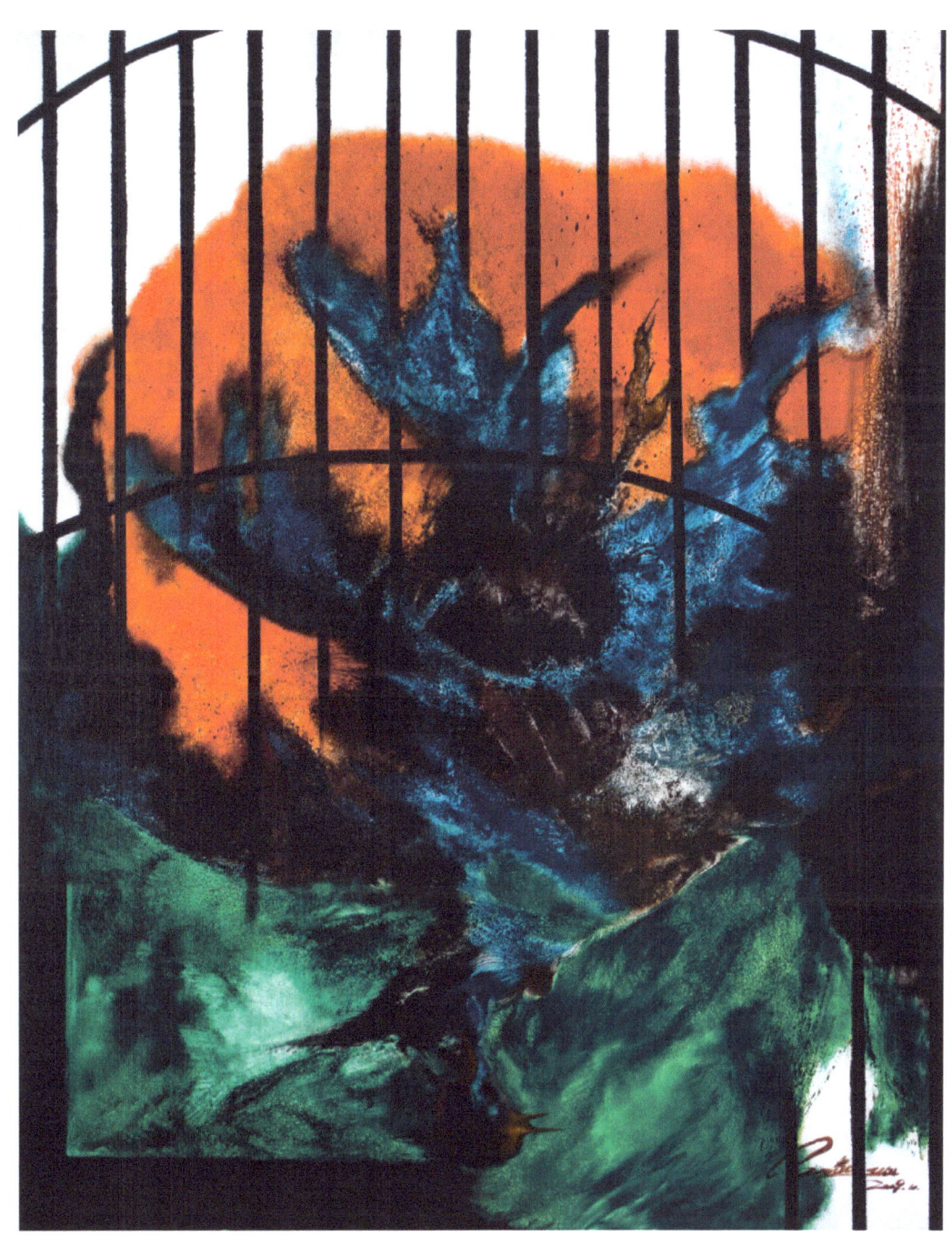

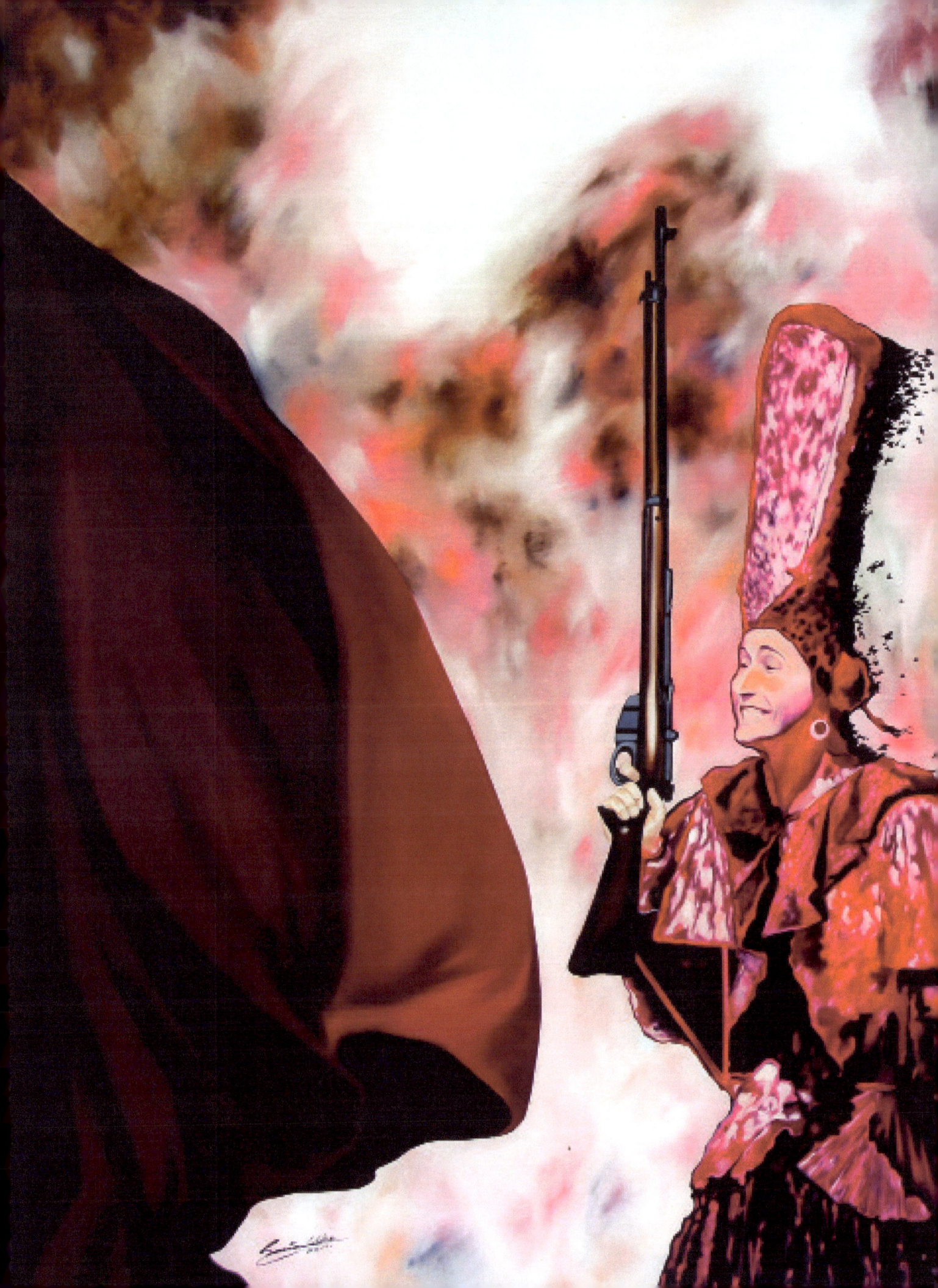

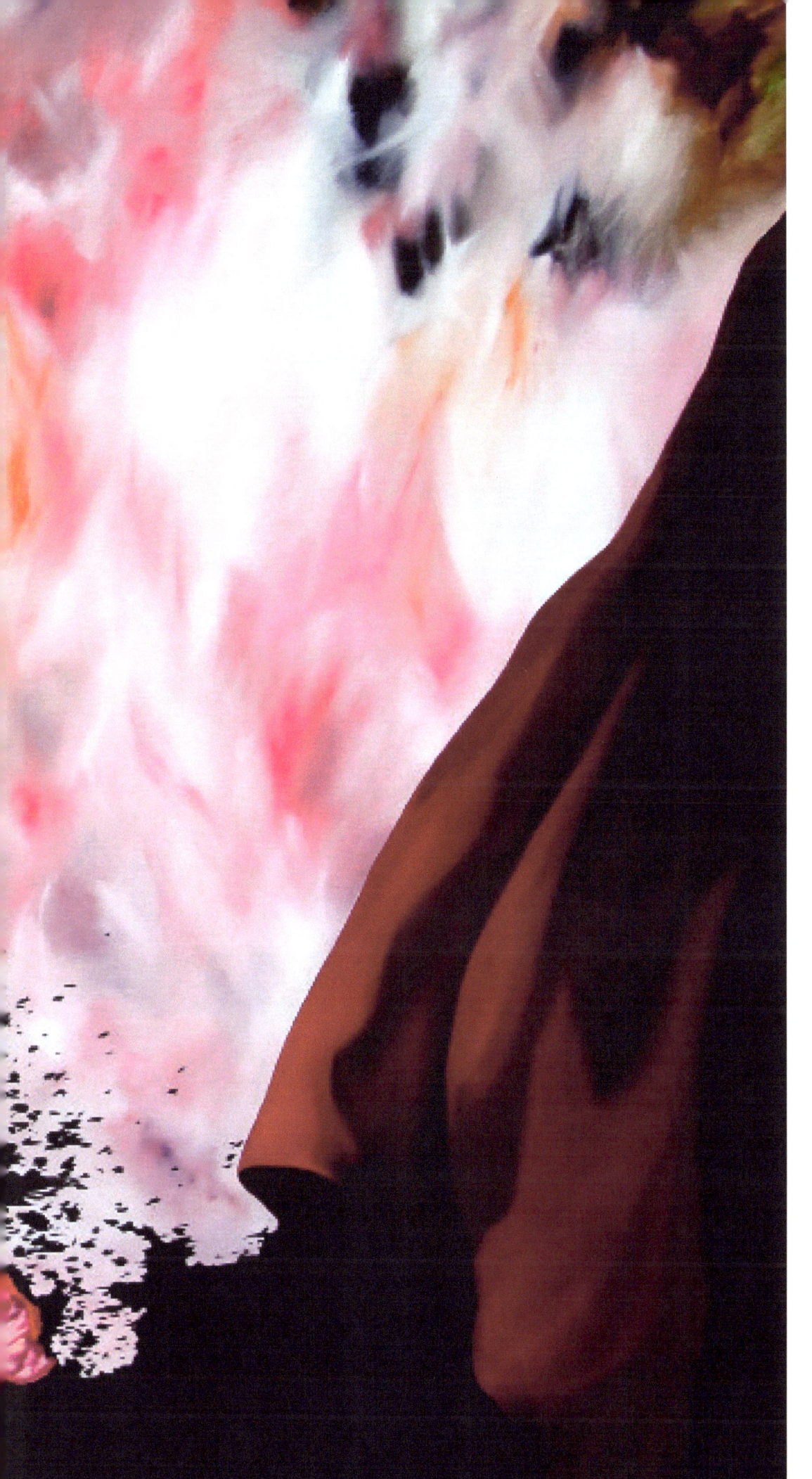

Each Party Oil on Canvas   15.7"   × 23.6"   2012

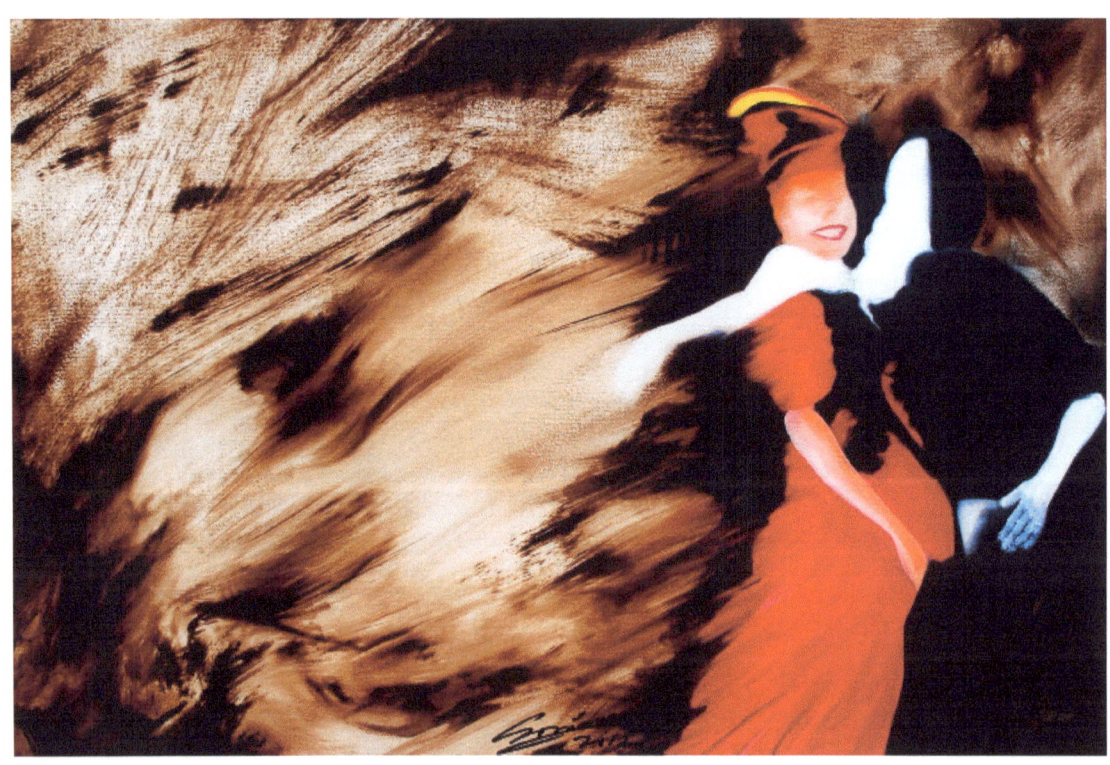

Manjusaka Oil on Canvas 19.7" ϕ 2011

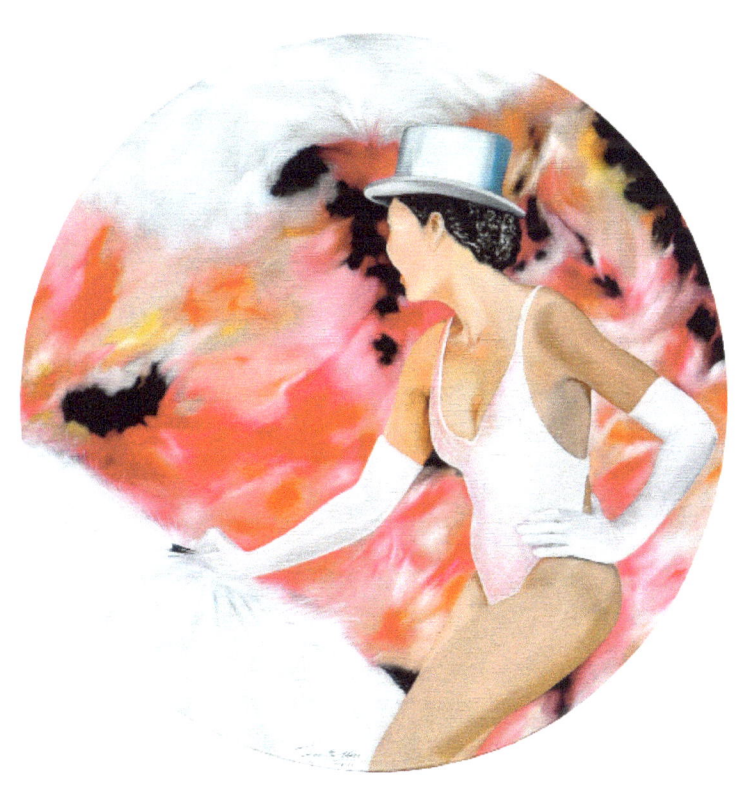

Perfect Irregularities Oil on Canvas

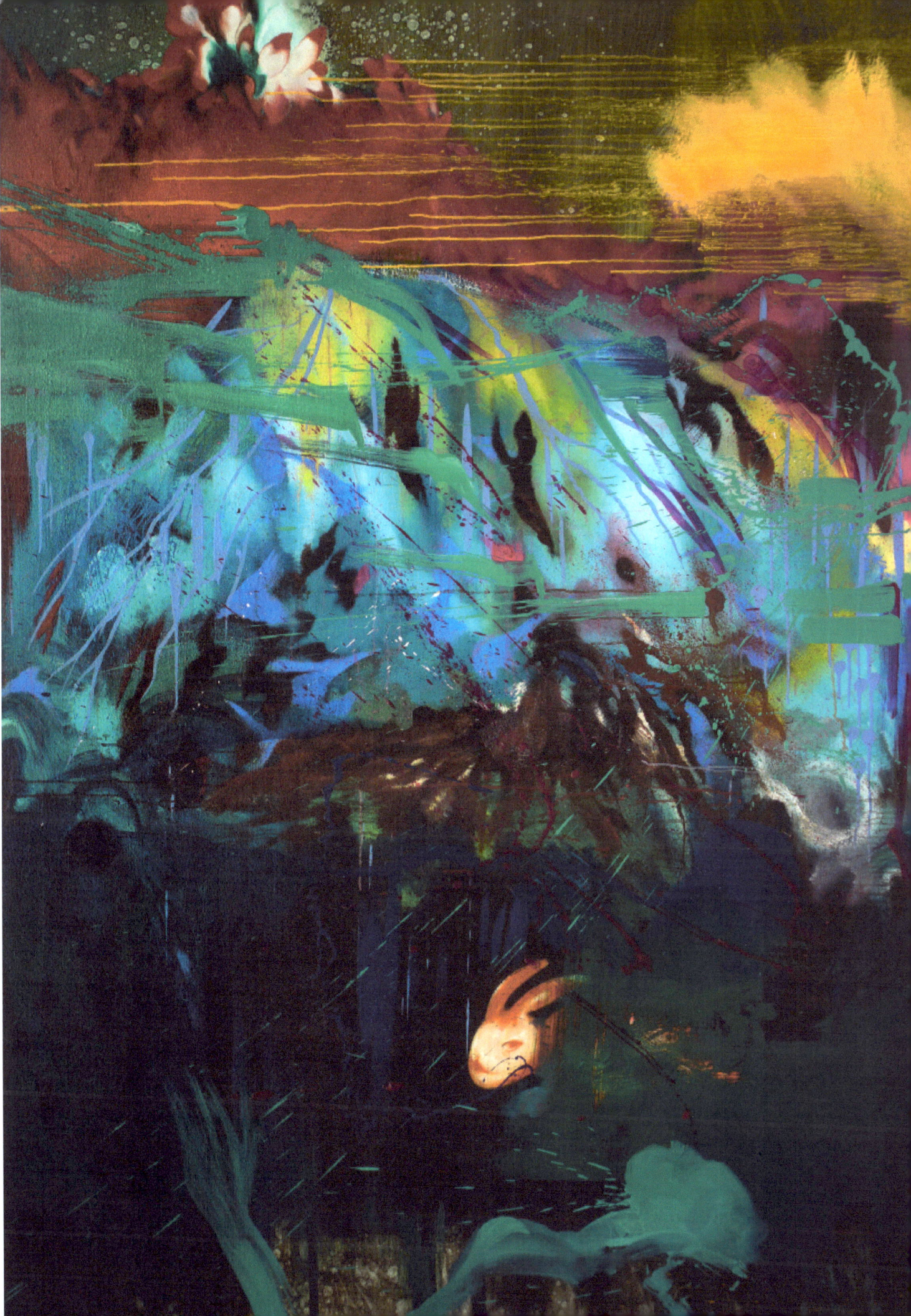

Pure Land Oil on Canvas   41.3"   × 41.3"   2013

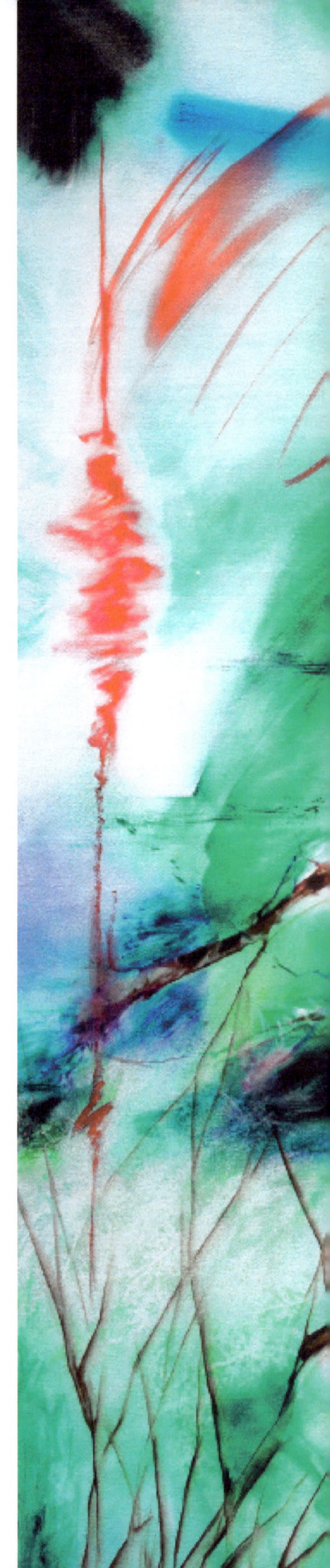

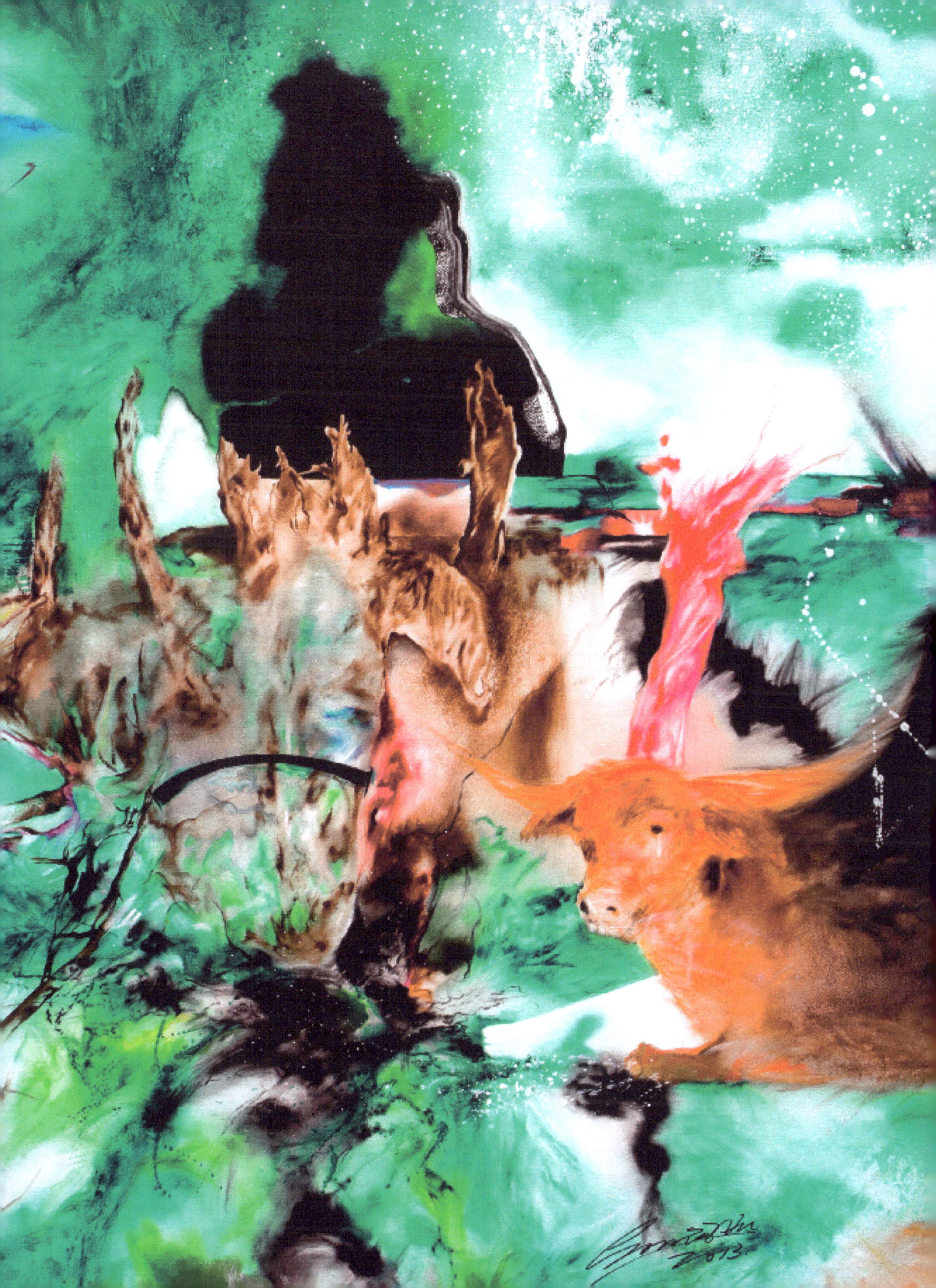

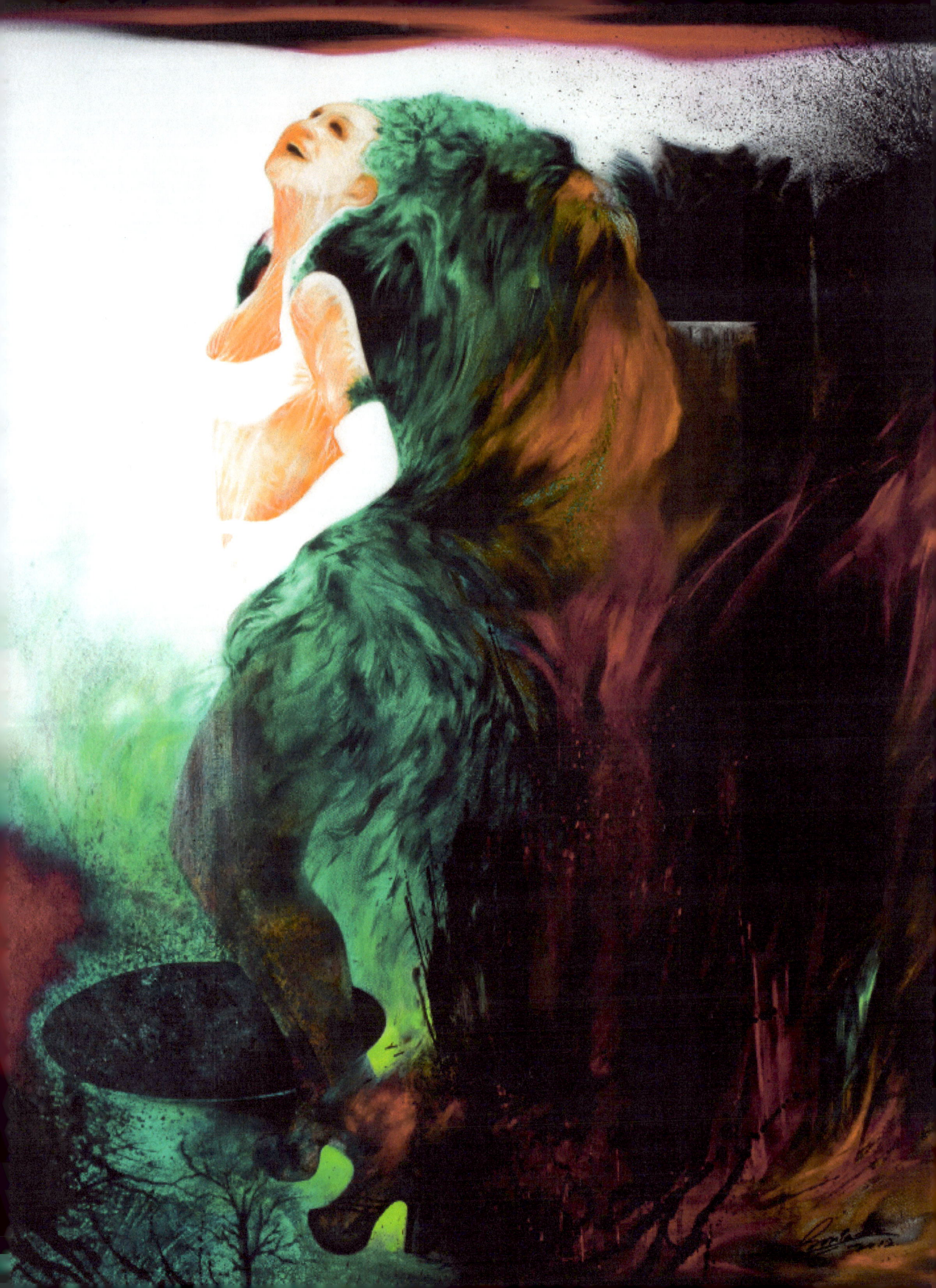

Graceful Oil on Canvas 47.2"   × 39.4" 2012

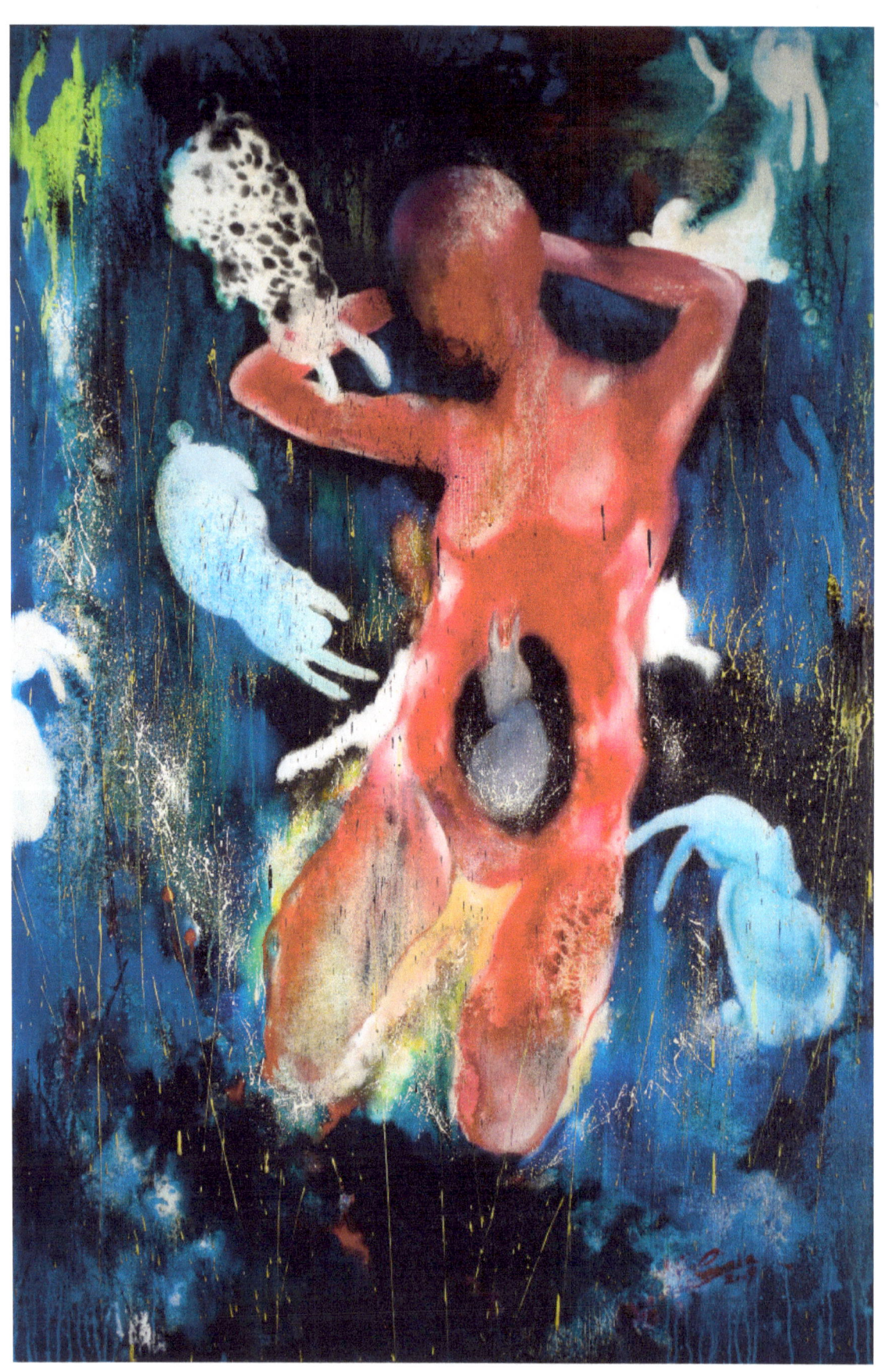

Cry Oil on Canvas 70.8" × 47.2" 2009